First steps in business training

First steps in business training

Vincent E. Collinge

Fourth Edition by
JOHN HARRISON, M.Inst.A.M., F.S.C.T., A.F.C.S.
Head of Department of Business Studies
Eastleigh Technical College

PITMAN

PITMAN BOOKS LIMITED
128 Long Acre, London WC2E 9AN

Associated Companies
Pitman Publishing Pty Ltd, Melbourne
Pitman Publishing New Zealand Ltd, Wellington

© Sir Isaac Pitman & Sons Ltd 1962, 1970, 1975

Fourth edition 1975, Reprinted 1977
Revised 1978, Reprinted 1979, 1980, 1981, 1982, 1983

Printed and bound in Great Britain
at The Pitman Press, Bath

ISBN 0 273 00897 8

Preface to the fourth edition

There has always been a need for a textbook to give junior commercial students a clear and concise treatment of basic business training. *First Steps in Business Training* is comprehensive without being exhaustive, simple in style, well provided with questions and facsimile forms, and reasonable in price; for these reasons it is thought that it will be especially suitable for students taking a business studies course at their school and for junior students at commercial and technical colleges.

The book is intended to be an introductory study of office work and commercial practice, and the subjects are those with which the junior office worker should be conversant so that she can efficiently play her part in the work of the office.

This new edition includes most aspects of office practice contained in the R.S.A. Stage I, Pitman Examinations Institute and C.S.E. Office Practice examination syllabuses. Questions set in office-practice examinations, including the more recent objective-type ones, have also been added, and I am grateful to the Royal Society of Arts for permission to reproduce these.

It has been necessary to restrict the number of questions given in this book in order to continue offering it at a reasonable price, but because of the emphasis now placed on assignments and practical examination questions I have made suitable references to those given in *Practical Office Exercises* which may be used to supplement the material supplied here.

J.H.

Contents

Section A: Office organization

The subjects dealt with in this section relate to the organization of an office. Office organization, so far as it concerns the junior office worker, entails dealing with incoming and outgoing post, using postal and remittance services, reproducing documents, taking messages, receiving callers and filing and indexing correspondence. These basic tasks should be understood by all who intend making a career in business.

Before the student begins her study of office work, however, she must know what is expected of her personally when she takes her place in an office. Seven very important rules of business etiquette are, therefore, given here for her guidance and observance:

1 *Be attentive* and alert. Listen attentively to instructions so that you need be told only once.

2 *Be neat* in your personal appearance and do not allow untidy work to pass out of your hands.

3 *Be orderly* in organizing your desk, equipment and cupboards and in planning out your daily work. Keep all of your personal belongings out of sight in a drawer or cupboard.

4 *Be punctual* at the office and in keeping all appointments.

5 *Be quiet* when working in the office, and be quiet, too, about business matters. Regard your work as confidential and do not discuss office matters with others.

6 *Be reliable* in carrying out *all* the routine tasks you are given to do.

7 *Be thorough* and ensure that every task you are given is satisfactorily completed and if you are in doubt about a spelling or an address, look it up in one of the reference books provided.

Message for

Mr. _G. H. Ellis_

WHILE YOU WERE OUT

Mr. _P. Spike_

OF _Melvin Manufacturing Co. Ltd._

TELEPHONE NO. _Linktown 416_

TELEPHONED	X	PLEASE RING	X
CALLED TO SEE YOU		WILL CALL AGAIN	
WANTS TO SEE YOU		URGENT	

MESSAGE: _Mr. Spike expects to be in the Leadington area next week, when he would like to call on you to discuss the matter referred to in your letter dated 3 January. Will you please ring him back today?_

DATE _5 Jan. 19_ TIME _09.30 hrs_

RECEIVED BY _Lorna Phipps_

Fig. 1 A telephone message sheet

Unit 1 Telephone messages and receiving callers

The office junior must realize how important it is to be absolutely reliable in taking messages for staff who are absent from their offices. An inaccurate message or a forgotten message can lead to the loss of an order and to other serious consequences.

Telephone messages

If a caller wishes to leave a message for someone who is out, the telephonist should make a note of the caller's name, business title, telephone number and of the details of the message in full. She should write the message down in her notebook while the caller is dictating it to her; on no account should she rely on her memory. She should then read back the full message to the caller and assure him that it will be given to the member of staff concerned. It should be written clearly or typed on a printed message sheet, as in Fig. 1, and the time and date of the call included as well as all the details noted during the telephone conversation. The completed message sheet should be signed and placed in a prominent position on the absent executive's desk.

Receiving callers

This is a duty which calls for personal qualities of tact and confidence. Here again, the junior is establishing an important 'first impression' and so she must see that the visitor has a pleasant and courteous greeting.

When she first meets the caller, the junior should make a note of his name, the name of his firm and a brief indication of the business to be discussed. These details may be entered in a Visitors' Book or Register of Callers, as in Fig. 2. She should then invite the caller to sit down in the waiting room while she contacts the appropriate member of staff and informs him of the caller's presence. If it is convenient for him to see the visitor, she conducts the latter to the office and makes the necessary introductions. On no account should callers be shown into an office before the member of staff has been informed.

REGISTER OF CALLERS

DATE	NAME OF CALLER	FIRM	TIME OF ARRIVAL	REFERRED TO
1 4 19-	J. Spellman	Spartan Electronics Ltd.	1030	Mr R Davis
-11-	P.A. Brown T. Coleman }	Olympica Ltd.	1100	Mrs J. Stainer
-11-	R. Patterson	Patterson & Sons	1400	Mr L Roberts

Fig. 2. Register of callers

Questions

1 If a telephone caller wishes to leave a message for someone who is out, what would you do?

2 Use a telephone-message form to record an urgent call, selecting the important information from the following details:

Mr Ray Adams of Gloucester Toys Limited phoned at 14.15 today before his area meeting re shortages of boxes for Mini-Kid range of toys. Owing to flooding of part of warehouse following a burst water main in Cheltenham Street all stocks of Mini-Kid boxes (code nos 2743641 to 2753652) damaged beyond repair. Could Mr Castle let him have emergency delivery of 300 of each box type, if possible within 72 hours; these boxes can be without labels which can follow. Mr Adams was phoning from the Highworth Street office of Gloucester Toys in Longlevens, Gloucester, and can be reached at 0452 713 extension 14. Mr Adams sent his regards and hopes to be visiting soon, after his trip to West Germany.   (R.S.A.)

3 If your duties included answering the telephone, what plan would you follow to make certain that all messages were delivered accurately and quickly? (R.S.A.)

4 On 5 June 19.., the following people called at the reception desk of Grosvenor Engineering Ltd:

Mr Roger Brook of B & C Electronics saw the Managing Director at 10.15 a.m. At 11.05 a.m. Miss V. Davids requested an appointment with the Personnel Department on private business.
The Marine Department received Mr C. Kavil of A. Peters Ltd at 4.00 p.m. Mr G. T. Robinson came at 9.30 a.m. for an appointment in the Diesel Department. (He is a representative of Tabco Ltd.)

Mr D. Samuels of Fitzroy Ltd arrived at 2.00 p.m. for an appointment in the Sales Department.

Enter the particulars of these callers, in the order in which they arrived, in a Register of Callers. Use the 24-hour time system. *(R.S.A.)*

5 Using the words given below write an account to describe the work of a receptionist in a busy office:

telephone	intercom	business card
diary	visitors' book	company literature
messages		*(R.S.A.)*

6 You are employed as a clerk-receptionist in a small engineering firm.

a What information would be recorded in your reception register?

b Why is it necessary to keep such a register?

c How would you deal with an office supplies sales representative who has called to see the chief buyer without appointment?

d What other duties might you be expected to carry out apart from reception?

(R.S.A.)

7 Select the correct answer below:

To ensure that a name in a telephone message is taken down correctly it is advisable to spell it out using the:

a loudspeaker;

b phonetic alphabet;

c ADC Service;

d *Post Office Guide.*

For additional practical questions, refer to Section 2.4 of *Practical Office Exercises.*

Unit 2 Incoming post

The work of opening and distributing the incoming post should be organized in such a way that the correspondence is on the desks of the staff responsible when they arrive at the office in the morning. A delay in distributing the morning's post can seriously affect the day's work and, therefore, a highly organized and efficient system is necessary, the following being one which is widely used today:

1 Business mail is sorted from mail marked 'Private' or 'Confidential'.
2 Open the business mail, take out the contents, open them flat and pin loose enclosures to the letters which they accompany.
3 Stamp every document with a date stamp, taking care not to obliterate important typewritten or printed matter on the correspondence. A rubber stamp giving the hour as well as the date of receipt may be used.
4 Extract all correspondence enclosing remittances and take the following action:

Remittances Book

Date	Remitter's Name	Method of Payment	Account No.	Amount £	Amount p	Signature
19--						
Jan. 1	Garfield, G.	Chq.	R.1162	11	00	
" 1	Palmer	Chq.	T.490	12	50	
" 1	Shell Garage	P.O.	R.1169		65	
" 1	Cox	Chq.	T.499	52	00	T. Jones.
" 1	London Engineering Co.	Chq.	P.1119	14	48	
" 1	Sanderson	Cash	P.1231	1	00	
" 1	Donald	Chq.	T.515	20	50	

Fig. 3. A remittances book

  a Check each remittance with the amount indicated on the correspondence and inform the chief clerk of any discrepancies.

  b Write the amount, method of payment (e.g. chq., P.O., or cash)
and your initials on the corner of the document.

  c Enter details of all remittances received in a remittances book (see
Fig. 3). Extract the remittances from the correspondence and hand
them to the chief cashier, who should sign for each item in the book.

5 The correspondence is now ready for sorting into departments or
sections, e.g. Sales, Export, Accounts, Secretarial, Works, Advertising,
Purchasing, Spares.

6 After the office manager has checked through the piles of correspondence, they are delivered to the managers of the offices concerned.

7 Private and confidential letters, which must not be opened, are
delivered to the addressees personally or to their private secretaries.

8 Recheck all envelopes to make sure that nothing has been left in them.

Letter-opening machine

A letter-opening machine may be used for cutting open the envelopes
received in the incoming mail (see Fig. 4). These machines are either
hand- or electrically-operated and, by a rotary blade or scissor action,
cut a strip off the edge of the envelope. Any size of envelope can be
accommodated up to a thickness of a quarter of an inch. These
machines are quick and efficient and, because only a very narrow strip
is cut from the envelopes, the contents are unlikely to be damaged.

Fig. 4. A letter-opening machine
(reproduced by permission of Roneo-Neopost Ltd)

Questions

1 Prepare a list of instructions to guide your junior in the opening and distribution of the incoming post during your absence on holiday.

2 Explain the uses of:

 a A letter-opening machine;
 b A date stamp.

3 Describe a system for controlling remittances received in the post.

4 Explain the uses of a remittances book and give a typical page with at least six entries.

5 The senior executives of your firm have complained that the morning's mail is late in being delivered from the mail room to their offices with a consequent delay in starting the day's business. The office manager has asked you to investigate the present method of handling the incoming mail and to devise a more satisfactory system which will not only ensure that the correspondence is available for distribution before the senior executives arrive in the morning, but will also take into account the need for security in the handling of remittances. Write a memorandum to the office manager setting out the procedure you would recommend. *(R.S.A.)*

6 Pair the following words, e.g. if you consider that (*a*) in the first column pairs with (*c*) in the second, write (*c*) against (*a*):

a Letter-opening machine	*a* Remittances book
b Reception	*b* Incoming post
c Cheques	*c* Outgoing post
d Franking machine	*d* Register of callers

For additional practical questions, refer to Section 1.6 of *Practical Office Exercises*.

Unit 3 Outgoing post

All outgoing post should pass through the following processes:

1 The letter is checked to see that enclosures are, where necessary, attached.
2 The address on the envelope is checked with the address on the letter. If there is a discrepancy, both the letter and the envelope should be returned to the typist for verification and re-typing.
3 The letter is folded, care being taken not to fold it more than is necessary to fit into its envelope.
4 The letter is placed in the envelope, which is sealed securely.
5 The envelope is weighed and postage stamps of the correct value are affixed to it.
6 Details from the envelope may be entered in a postage book.
7 First-class letters should be separated from second-class letters when posting.
8 The envelope is posted.

Enclosures

A document which is attached to a letter is referred to as an 'enclosure'. The typist may use any of the following methods to indicate on the letter that there is an enclosure:

1 Type 'Enc.' at the bottom of the letter.
2 Type / (called the solidus) in the margin in line with the sentence which refers to the enclosure.
3 An enclosure label may be affixed to the letter or numbered labels can be issued in duplicate (one copy is affixed to the enclosure and one to the letter).

The postage book

A postage book may be used to record particulars of postal packets dispatched. It contains a record of all letters posted and is a check on the postage stamps used. The cashier advances a round sum, say £5, for the purchase of stamps by the junior who is responsible for the outgoing post. This amount is entered in the left-hand 'Stamps Bought' column. The postage book is balanced every day, i.e. the total value of the postage stamps used is subtracted from the value of the cash received plus any stamps brought forward from the previous day, and the result should give the value of the postage stamps in hand. A specimen page of a postage book is given in Fig. 5.

If a detailed postage book is not used, the postal clerk will be required to keep a daily record of the total stamps used. The postage book will also not be necessary if a franking machine is in use, as the machine meter indicates the amount of postage used.

Stamps Bought		Details of Name and Town	Units Used		Remarks
£	P		£	P	
		13th February 19--			
1	22	*Balance b/f*			
5	00	*Cash paid*			
		Underwood London		10	
		Turner Crewe.		8	
		Cartwrights Sons Oxford		50	*Registered*
		Smith Oxford.		8	
		Circular to area Representatives	2	56	*32 @ 8p*
		Peters London		10	
		Gardens London		8	
		Crewe Bros. Oxford		8	
		Pheasant Oxford		60	*Parcel.*
			4	18	
		Balance c/f	2	04	
6	22		6	22	
		14th February 19--			
2	04	*Balance b/f*			

Fig. 5. Specimen page of a postage book

Collection of mail by the Post Office

Instead of the office junior having to deliver large quantities of mail to the Post Office, arrangements can be made for a postman to collect it from the office, provided the following quantities are being dispatched:

1   First- and second-class letters, when the number amounts to 1,000 or the total postage amounts to £35.

2 Ordinary parcels where the number at any one time is 100 or more.
3 The Post Office will make a regular collection of ordinary parcels if
   there is at least twenty at a time.

   These services are provided without charge, but it should be noted that
   the Post Office usually requires three hours' notice; application for free
   collection may be made in person, in writing or by telephone.

Questions

1 Rule up a postage book for 13 February 19.., enter the following items and
   balance it at the end of the day: £

Balance b/f		0.70
Cash received		5.00
Lennon	London	0.08
Smart	Oxford	0.10
Brown & Sons	Reading	0.70 Parcel
Andrews	Birmingham	0.08
Thompson	London	0.60 Registered
Williams	Manchester	0.08
Circular to Branch Managers	25 @ 8p	
Palmer, Smith & Co.	London	0.10

2 What is an enclosure? How are enclosures indicated on letters?

3 Explain the arrangements which can be made for the collection of letters and
   parcels by the Post Office.

4 You work in the office of a small firm, and you are responsible for recording
   expenditure on postage. Would you think it necessary to enter every item
   separately? Give a specimen ruling of a postage book and make ten entries.
   (R.S.A.)

5 One of your responsibilities is the packing and posting of mail. What steps
   will you take to ensure that the job is done satisfactorily?   *(R.S.A.)*

6 Use the terms given below to complete the diagram on page 12 which shows
   the sequence of dealing with outgoing mail in a large office:

weigh if necessary	parcels
frank	letters – first class
wrap	outgoing mail
sort	label
weigh	letters – second class *(R.S.A.)*

For additional practical questions, refer to Section 1.3 of *Practical Office
Exercises.*

ORGANISATION OF OUTGOING MAIL

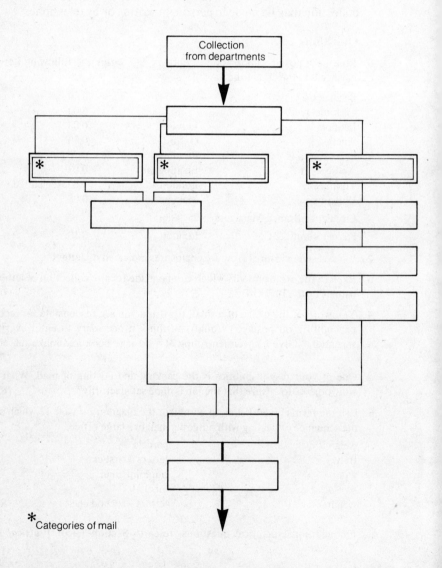

* Categories of mail

Unit **4** Postal-room equipment

Offices handling large quantities of mail find it quicker and more economical to introduce mechanization into several of their postal-room processes. Machinery is, for example, used for:

1 Folding papers.
2 Collating papers.
3 Opening envelope flaps and inserting papers.
4 Sealing envelopes.
5 Printing postal impressions.
6 Counting and stacking the envelopes.

Postal-franking machine

I shall describe the postal-franking machine in detail, as it is the postal machine most commonly found in offices.

The postal-franking machine is used to print postal impressions on envelopes. If one of these machines is used, the clerk no longer has the unpleasant and unhygienic task of sticking adhesive stamps to the packages. All types of mail can be franked, including ordinary letter post, registered letters, telegrams, overseas mail and parcels.

Franking machines are either hired or purchased from the manufacturers but, before they can be put into use, a licence has to be obtained from the local head postmaster. The user must pay in advance for the postage units and the machine has to be presented at a specified Post Office for meter setting or registering.

A lever or knob is set to the required postal value and when the handle is operated the envelope is passed through the machine and an impression is made. The impression gives the date, postal district, value and, if desired, an advertisement or the user's name and address, as illustrated in Fig. 6. Every time the machine prints an impression, the number of units is recorded on the meter. The value of the credit on hand is calculated by subtracting the number of units used from the number of units purchased. Both amounts are shown on the machine.

If a package is too thick to pass through the machine, a strip of gummed label can be franked and affixed to it.

Fig. 6. A franking impression

The postal clerk is responsible for changing the date on the machine, cleaning the type and replenishing the supply of red dye as and when required.

When all of the post has been franked it must be securely tied in bundles with the names and addresses all facing the same way and handed over the counter of a Post Office or posted in a specially-prepared envelope. A franking-machine control card must be submitted to the Post Office at the end of every week. This form shows:

1 Name of firm.
2 Meter office, i.e. the name of the Post Office where the machine is registered.
3 Registered number of the machine.
4 Setting or recording unit.
5 Reading of ascending register at close of business on every day of the week, i.e. the number of units used.
6 The daily reading of the descending register for a locking machine or the last entry on the record card for a non-locking machine.
7 Signature of the postal clerk.
8 Date.

The daily entry must be made on completion of each day's postings.

A specimen franking-machine control card illustrating the above points is given in Fig. 7.

Any envelopes franked in error should be retained and submitted to the Post Office, which will issue a refund for the value of the impressions less a charge of 5 per cent.

Folding machine

Where large quantities of circulars, invoices, statements, price lists, etc. have to be folded for the post, a folding machine may be used. Folding machines, which may be operated by hand or electrically, are

FRANKING MACHINE CONTROL CARD

Licensee Barrington Builders Limited

Machine (or Meter No.) E 1923 — Setting or Recording Unit ½p

Meter Office (as shown on Record Card) Hereford P.O.

I certify that the following entries for the above machine for the week ended 4 June 19— are correct and that the correct date has been shown on each day's posting

CHECK DATE DAILY 28

Put initials in column below to show date has been changed		ALL MACHINES: Reading of Ascending Register (Totalisator)	LOCKING MACHINES: Reading of Descending Register (Credit Meter)	ALL MACHINES: Last entry in col. "Total Deposits" or "Total Settings" on Record Card
PB	Mon.	14962		16500
PB	Tue.	15101		16500
PB	Wed.	17232		21500
PB	Thur.	17999		21500
PB	Fri.	19127		21500
	Sat.			

NOTE 1. Whether or not the machine has been used, **this** card must be posted on Saturday, or on Friday if no postings are made on Saturday.

NOTE 2. The daily entry must be made on completion of each day's postings.

Signed P. Brown

4 June 19—

Post Office Examining Officer's initials ……………

Fig. 7. A franking-machine control card
(*reproduced by permission of the Post Office*)

capable of making up to three folds. The papers are automatically fed into the machine and the position of the folds is changed by adjusting a lever or knob on a setting scale.

Envelope-sealing machine

An envelope-sealing machine is capable of moistening the gum and sealing the flaps on envelopes. The envelopes are fed automatically into the machine and the process, which is quick and hygienic, enables large quantities to be sealed securely.

Collating machine

A collating machine enables the operator to sort and collate documents easily and quickly. Instead of the pages being spread out over a table, they are fitted into a collating cabinet. The compact arrangement of the paper containers in the machine eliminates a great deal of the fatigue normally experienced when papers are collated from a table.

Inserting and mailing machine

This machine, which is only suitable for offices handling circularized mail on a large scale, is capable of:

1 Collating up to eight enclosures.
2 Opening the envelope flap.
3 Inserting enclosures into the envelope.
4 Moistening the flap.
5 Sealing the envelope.
6 Printing the postal impression on to the envelope.
7 Counting and stacking the envelopes.

Questions

1 Describe the procedure for maintaining and controlling a postal-franking machine.

2 *(a)* Enter the following details on a franking-machine control card:

Name: Town Clerk's Dept, Sinderton
Meter office: Sinderton P.O.
Unit: $^{1}/_{2}$p Machine No. B.1267
Number of units used: 72 496
Number of units purchased: 80 000

(b) What was the balance of credit at the end of the day?

3 You are employed in the mailing department of a large organization. Name three machines which would simplify and speed up the handling of incoming and outgoing mail. Describe these machines and their functions.   *(R.S.A.)*

4 Select the correct answer below:

A machine which assembles pages into the required order is called:

a a collator;
b a franking machine;
c a paper knife;
d a fingerette.   *(R.S.A.)*

For additional practical questions, refer to Section 1.2 of *Practical Office Exercises.*

Unit 5 Inland postal services

The office junior should be conversant with the various inland postal services offered by the Post Office. These comprise:

1 First-class letters and cards.
2 Second-class letters and cards.
3 Parcels.
4 Second-class letters posted in bulk.
5 Newspapers.
6 Express services:

    a Express all the way;
    b Special delivery;
    c Railex

7 Railway services:

    a Letters;
    b Parcels.

8 Airway letters.
9 Business-reply service.
10 Freepost.
11 Methods of collecting mail:

    a Private boxes;
    b Private bags;
    c Poste Restante.

12 Certificates of posting.
13 Recorded-delivery service.
14 Datapost.

A brief description is given below of each of these services, but it should be noted that the full regulations and current charges are set out in the *Post Office Guide*. This reference book should always be available in the mailing room for quick reference. Amendment notices are issued by the Post Office from time to time and it is usually the responsibility of the office junior to see that these are incorporated in the current issue of the *Post Office Guide*.

Letters and cards

Letters and cards may be sent by first-class and second-class services. Second-class letters will normally be delivered up to one working day later than first-class except that, over long or difficult journeys, they may take a little longer. The class of a letter is determined by the amount of postage paid; no written indication of service is necessary. The printed-paper service has been discontinued and all letters may now be sealed. There is a weight limit of $1\frac{1}{2}$ lb for second-class letters, but there is no weight limit for first-class letters. A letter if posted unpaid, except in the business-reply and freepost services, is treated as a second-class letter, and is charged on delivery with double second-class postage; a letter posted with less than second-class postage is treated as a second-class letter and charged with double the amount of the deficit of second-class postage.

Parcels

The maximum weight for a parcel is 22 lb and it must not be more than 3 ft 6 in. in length, or 6 ft length and girth combined. Parcels posted to an address in the local parcel-delivery area, i.e. those postal addresses having the same post town as that of the office of posting, have a small reduction of postage. The address should be written on the parcel itself and not merely on a label, which may become detached. In case the wrapping becomes damaged, or the parcel cannot be delivered, the sender's address should appear both inside the parcel and on the cover. On the cover it should be kept distinct from, and should preferably be to the left of and at right-angles to, the name and address of the addressee. The parcel should be marked 'Parcel Post' and handed to the appropriate officer at the counter of a Post Office; the sender, who must himself affix the postage stamps, should see that the weight, size and postage are in order before leaving.

The Postage Forward Parcel Service enables a person or firm to receive parcels from clients without prepayment of postage; the postage, with a small fee on each parcel, being paid by the addressee. This service is designed for the needs of businesses who wish to obtain a parcel from a client without putting him to the expense of paying postage.

A certificate of posting may be obtained, for a small charge, for un-registered parcels and, where large numbers of parcels are dispatched

```
INLAND PARCEL POST                                           PP 90B

LIST OF PARCELS POSTED

Name of Poster  J. Thompson                    Date  2c/3/19 -

FULL NAME AND ADDRESS AS SHOWN ON THE PARCEL

(For COD parcels the sender should keep a record of the numbers of the relative
  Trade Charge Forms)

 1  Fraynot T.P.   14 High Street,  Worcester WR1 4TR
 2  Williams Bros  29 Park Road  Cardiff CF8 9CP
 3  Kirby G.       101A Regent Street,  London W1 1DW
 4  Reynolds Engineering Ltd  Park Trading Estate  Leeds L1 2RX
 5  Potterton & Granger Bros  The Triangle  Leeds L1 4AS
 6  Ford L.M.      80 The Highway,  Worcester WR1 5AS
 7
 8
 9
10
11
12
13
14
15
16
17
18
19
20
```

NOTE: In the event of loss, damage or delay, this list will confer no title to compensation.

Postage stamps (or franking machine impression) to the value of 1p for each parcel (up to a maximum of 10p per posting) to be affixed here by the sender.

Date Stamp

Accepting Officers initials

56-7694 McC

Fig. 8. A parcel-receipt book

(*reproduced by permission of the Post Office*)

daily, a parcels book will normally be used for listing the names and addresses and obtaining a collective receipt. Fig. 8 illustrates the type of form used for this purpose.

Second-class letters posted in bulk

Rebates of postage are allowed on second-class letters posted in bulk (4,251 is the minimum number) for delivery in Great Britain and Northern Ireland. The rebate must be applied for in advance of posting on a special form obtainable from a Head Post Office. The packets must all be originated by the same sender and must be identical in shape, in size and in the nature of their contents, and must be available for posting all at the same time or in batches as the local Head Postmaster requires. They should be sorted into geographical divisions and securely tied, with their addresses all arranged in the same direction, in bundles of fifty. Further details of the conditions and amounts of rebate are given in the *Post Office Guide.*

Newspapers

Copies of publications which have been registered as newspapers at the Post Office are eligible for transmission by the inland newspaper post and are given the same service as first-class letters. They must be posted by the publishers or their agents and prominently marked 'Newspaper Post'. All other newspapers are transmitted as first- or second-class letters.

Express services

Express all the way

A packet which is sent by this service is conveyed all the way by Post Office messenger, for which a charge per mile is made. The word 'Express' must be boldly and legibly written above the address in the left-hand corner of the cover and the packet must be handed over the counter of a Post Office. After delivering an express packet, a messenger may accept a reply or perform a further express service within the authorized hours. The fees can be paid either by the sender of the original service or by the sender of the reply and will be charged for on the same basis as an original service. A sender desiring a reply after his packet has been delivered should write the words 'Wait Reply' above the address on the packet.

Special delivery

Under this service the sender of a postal packet may arrange for a special delivery by messenger after the packet's arrival at the office of delivery, provided that it arrives at a time when messengers are available. The packet is dispatched from the office of posting by the next ordinary mail and is specially picked out from the rest both at the delivery office and at any intermediate office through which it may have to pass. A special delivery fee is payable in addition to the first-class letter postage. Letters may be handed in at a Post Office, given to a postman in a rural district or, unless intended for registration, may be posted in a letter box. A broad blue or black line must be drawn from top to bottom on both the front and back of the letter.

Railex

Under this service, which is available when messengers are on duty, any Post Office which is an express-delivery office will accept an un-registered packet, convey it to the appropriate railway station, and dispatch it by the next available train to the station of destination. A messenger will meet the train and deliver the packet to its address provided that it arrives during the hours when the messengers are on duty.

Railway services

Letters

These are conveyed by the first available train from the railway station where they are handed in, and:

1 Transferred on arrival to the nearest Post Office letter box, or
2 Left at the station of destination to be called for.

The sender may arrange for a Post Office messenger to meet the train at the station of destination and deliver the letter. Postage at first-class letter rate must be prepaid by means of stamps affixed to the cover in the normal way. In addition the railway fee, which must be paid in cash at the railway station, is payable on each letter.

Parcels

A railway parcel may be handed in at an express-delivery Post Office and taken by a Post Office messenger to the nearest railway station for dispatch by the first available train. The sender must find out and pay the amount of the railway charges for conveying the parcel, and the messenger hands over the sum received to the railway official when he delivers it to the station. The sender may also arrange, by preparing and dispatching a telegram to the express-delivery Post Office nearest the station of destination, for a Post Office messenger to call at the station, collect the parcel and deliver it to its address, in which case the words 'Railway Parcel, to be handed to Post Office Messenger at . . . station' must be written on the cover.

Airway letters

On certain air routes operated by British Airways, airway letters are carried by the first available direct air service from the airline's air terminal or town terminal where they are handed in. On arrival at their destination, they are either left at the airport or town terminal to be called for, or transferred from the town terminal to the ordinary post. The maximum weight which can be carried is 1 lb, and this service is not available to the Irish Republic or to any country overseas.

Business reply

Under this service, a person who wishes to obtain a reply from a client without putting him to the expense of paying postage may enclose in his communication an unstamped reply card, letter card, envelope, folder or gummed label of a special design. He may also incorporate in his advertisements in newspapers and other publications a special design to be used as an address label or as a folder. The client can post the card, etc., in the ordinary way, but without a stamp, and the addressee will pay the usual postage together with a fee on each item. A licence to use the service must be obtained from the Post Office.

Freepost

This is a similar service to business reply except that special envelopes or cards are not used and the user merely quotes a special address. Replies bearing this address can then be posted in the ordinary way, but only as second-class, and without stamps and the addressee pays the postage on all the replies he receives, plus a small fee on each item.

Methods of collecting mail

Private boxes

Instead of the mail being delivered in the ordinary way, a private box may be rented at a Post Office for the reception of postal packets 'to be called for' by the renter or his agent. The box must be taken for a definite address in the postal district in which the service is required and letters and parcels addressed to the renter must bear his full address and include the private box number, e.g.

> Messrs. John Payne & Sons
> P.O. Box No. 149
> 21 Bolton Street
> BLANKTOWN
> BN8 3AP

By means of this service the renter can obtain his mail before the normal delivery time. Correspondence is handed over only on production of a check card.

Private bags

A private bag may be used for the posting and receipt of correspondence. The bag, which must be conveyed by the user or his agent, is locked at the Post Office before it is handed over.

Poste restante

Poste Restante means post waiting. To assist travellers with no fixed address, correspondence and parcels may be addressed to them at all Post Offices, except town sub-offices. The words 'Post Restante' or 'To be Called for' must be included in the address. At the expiry of two weeks (one month for a packet originating at a place abroad) postal packets are treated as undeliverable.

To ensure delivery to the right person addressees must, when calling for mail, produce evidence of their identity.

Certificates of posting

For a small charge a certificate of posting can be obtained for an unregistered letter, the fee being payable by means of a postage stamp affixed by the sender to the certificate. It provides proof that a packet has been posted to a particular person, but in the event of loss or damage it does not entitle the sender to compensation. A single certificate can be obtained for several postal packets of the same kind posted at the same time if a list of the names and addresses is presented with them.

Recorded-delivery service

The recorded-delivery service is designed for the correspondent who requires not only proof of posting but, if necessary, proof of delivery. The package must be handed in at a Post Office and not posted in a posting box. The sender completes a recorded-delivery form, detaches the numbered gummed label and sticks it on the packet above and to the left of the address. He must also stamp the packet for the normal postage, plus the fee for recorded delivery. The sender hands the packet and the certificate to the Post Office counter clerk, who initials and date-stamps the certificate and returns it to the sender.

The packages are carried in the ordinary unregistered mail, but the delivery postman enters in a special book the serial number of the label on the letter or packet. On delivery he asks the addressee or recipient to sign against the number in the book. The delivery Post Office keeps the receipt book, and if the sender wishes to obtain a certificate of delivery, he fills in an advice of delivery form (obtainable at any Post Office). He must attach a postage stamp if requested at the time of posting or a stamp for an additional fee if requested at a later date.

Recorded delivery can be used for all kinds of inland postal packets, except parcels, railex packets, airway letters, railway letters and parcels and cash on delivery packets. Compensation up to £2 is payable for loss of a recorded-delivery package, but this service may not be used for money, packets containing jewellery, or any other contents with a total cash value of more than £2.

Datapost

This service provides for the overnight delivery of packages containing computer data; it is a door-to-door service for firms who use computers which are remote from their own premises. Packages are collected at agreed times and delivered to the computer at a pre-arranged time next morning. Charges are negotiated on the basis of a contract, taking into account weight, destination and timing of collection and delivery.

Questions

1   How does one obtain a certificate of posting? Does such a certificate entitle the holder to compensation in the event of the loss of a postal packet for which a certificate has been obtained?   *(R.S.A.)*

2   When would you expect to use the following services:
   a Poste restante;
   b Railex;
   c Freepost?

3   What are the advantages of renting a private box?

4   Which Post Office services would you use in each of the following instances:
   a to enable customers in this country to reply to you without having to pay postage;
   b to convey an urgent parcel required the same day in a town about 200 miles away;
   c to send a legal document in which proof of delivery may be required in a court of law;
   d to obtain correspondence in advance of the normal time of delivery;
   e to dispatch computer tape to a computer at the firm's head office about 100 miles away?   *(R.S.A.)*

5   In each of the two parts of this question, select the correct answer:
   (i)   A parcel to be collected by a traveller who has no fixed address would be sent:
      a Recorded delivery;
      b Poste restante;
      c C.O.D.;
      d Railex.
   (ii) The business-reply service can be used:
      a only by a firm possessing a franking machine;
      b by a firm wishing a customer to pay for the postage of a reply;
      c only by a firm possessing an addressing machine;
      d by a firm wishing to pay the postage of a customer's reply.   *(R.S.A.)*

For additional practical questions, refer to Sections 1.4 and 1.7 of *Practical Office Exercises.*

Unit 6 Overseas postal services

A description of overseas postal services, including the rates of postage, limits of weight, customs declaration forms required, prohibitions and restrictions, frequency of service and approximate times of transmission from London, is given separately for each country in the *Post Office Guide*. The current rates of airmail services are given in the *Airmail Leaflet*, which is published monthly and may be obtained free of charge from any Post Office.

The principal postal services available to destinations abroad include:

Surface mail	*Airmail*
Ordinary letter post	Ordinary letter post
Postcards	Air letter forms
Printed papers	Postcards
Small packets	Printed papers
Parcels	Newspapers
Cash on delivery	Small packets
	Parcels

Letters to Europe

Letters and postcards for European destinations go automatically by air or surface mail, whichever is the quicker. The payment of airmail postage is unnecessary and airmail labels should not be used. This is known as the 'all-up' service.

Small packets

This service provides for the transmission of goods, whether dutiable or not, in the same mails as printed papers which, as a rule, travel more quickly than parcels. The sender must write his name and address on the outside of the packet and must write the words 'Small Packet' in the top left-hand corner on the address side of the packet. The packets must be wrapped in such a way that they may be easily examined without any seal being broken. Letters, notes or documents having the character of current and personal correspondence may not be sent in a small packet.

Airmail

Blue airmail labels should be affixed to all airmail packages, except those destined for Europe.

Air-letter forms

These may be sent to any address in the world. They must not contain enclosures and must be written on either the stamped air-letter forms which are obtainable from Post Offices, or on privately-manufactured forms on which the postage may be prepaid either by means of the necessary postage stamp or by a franking-machine impression.

Printed papers

Printed papers, including printed and duplicated circulars, may be sent by the reduced printed-paper rate of postage provided that they do not contain letters or any message that constitutes personal correspondence. They must be packed in unsealed envelopes or in such a way that they may be easily examined without breaking any seal.

Customs declaration forms

All packages for places abroad are liable to be opened for examination in the country of destination and the contents are subject to the customs and other legal requirements of the country.

Two kinds of customs declaration forms are in use:

1 An adhesive form to be affixed to the package.
2 A non-adhesive form, of which two or more copies may be required. With non-adhesive forms a dispatch note is also required.

Details of the number and type of customs declaration forms to be used are given separately for each country in the *Post Office Guide*. The sender of a parcel must make an accurate declaration of the nature and value of the contents. Customs declaration forms can be obtained beforehand from any Post Office which accepts parcels for abroad. The forms should be filled up in ink, and senders are recommended to avoid the use of abbreviations, ditto marks, etc., which may not be intelligible in the country of destination. If the contents are not fully described or are undervalued, the parcel is liable to seizure and penalties may be incurred.

All packets posted for abroad at the *letter rate* of postage and containing goods, whether or not dutiable in the country of destination, must be declared to customs. If the value of the goods does not exceed

£50 a green label form of declaration is sufficient, but for goods in excess of £50 or if the goods are sent by the insured box service a non-adhesive declaration form should be used.

Reply coupons

An International reply coupon may be used to prepay a reply to a letter sent abroad. Instead of the writer enclosing a stamped addressed envelope he encloses a reply coupon which the addressee exchanges for postage stamps at a Post Office abroad.

Questions

1 Your firm receives many inquiries from overseas customers. What types of postal services are available for the dispatch overseas of letters, literature and samples? *(R.S.A.)*

2 How would you send dutiable articles by letter post?

3 Calculate the amount of postage for the items given below:

Item	Weight	Amount of postage
Letter (first-class)	3¾ oz *45g*	
Postcard (not urgent)	–	
Business-reply letter	¾ oz *30g*	
Airway letter	3½ oz *50g*	
Air-letter form	–	
Parcel	10 lb *4·2kg*	
Postcard (urgent)	–	
Express letter (express all the way)	½ oz – 5 miles *50g*	
Printed papers sent by second-class	7 oz *225g*	
First-class letter and certificate of posting	4½ oz *125g*	
Letter (second-class)	15 oz *450g*	
Parcel	5½ lb *3½kg*	
Railway letter	1½ oz *40g*	
Reply coupon (International)	–	
Express letter (special delivery)	1½ oz *35g*	

Item	Weight	Amount of postage
Letter to Europe	³/₄ oz 60g	
Newspaper	15¹/₂ oz 425g	
Railex	14 oz 450g	

4 Select the correct answer below:

   The 'all-up' service applies to:

   a letters and postcards for Europe;
   b increased rates of postage in the United Kingdom;
   c letters and postcards for countries outside Europe;
   d H.M. Forces outside Europe.

   For additional practical questions, refer to Section 1.1 of *Practical Office Exercises.*

Unit **7** Postal remittances

The following Post Office remittance services are available for the transmission of money by post:

1 Postage stamps.
2 Registration.
3 Postal orders.
4 Telegraphic money orders.
5 Cash on delivery.
6 National Giro.

Postage stamps

Postage stamps may be used for the payment of very small amounts, such as for brochures, competition fees, small items ordered by post or for refunding small amounts. This form of payment would not normally be used for amounts exceeding 10p.

Registration

The registration service can be used for transmitting sums of money and other valuables up to a maximum of £600. The amount of the registration fee varies according to the value of the articles sent. The fees payable and the compensation allowed can be found in the *Post Office Guide*.

Registered letters must be handed over the counter of a Post Office and a certificate of posting, bearing an acknowledgement that the fee for registration has been paid, must be obtained. The packages must be fastened with wax, gum or any other adhesive substance; it is not sufficient merely to tie them with string, but if this is used in addition to wax, etc., the string need not be sealed. Packages are also acceptable if they are secured by means of a lead, steel or strong metal seal crushed with a press. Whatever method of fastening or sealing is adopted, it is essential that it should not be possible to remove any part of the contents of the letter or parcel without either breaking or tearing the case, wrapper or cover or forcing two adhesive surfaces apart or breaking a seal. If a package is fastened by means of strips of adhesive paper or tape, each strip must bear stamped or printed on it some mark or word distinctive of the sender such as his initials or name, or must be signed or initialled by him or the person who tenders the packet for registration. Ordinary envelopes and parcels must be marked with a vertical and horizontal blue line on the back and front of the packet. Money sent by registered post must be enclosed in one of the registered-letter envelopes sold by the Post Office. Coins must be packed in such a way that they cannot move about inside the envelope.

If several registered packets are sent at the same time they should be accompanied by a list in duplicate of the names and addresses; one list is retained at the Post Office and the other, when completed and signed by the Post Office clerk, is returned to the sender.

For a further fee, the sender of a registered packet may arrange for an advice of delivery to be sent to him.

The compensation fee parcels service provides for compensation up to £200 for loss or damage to parcels. The sender must complete a certificate of posting with the addressee's name and address and the amount of compensation required and hand it to the Post Office counter clerk together with the parcel, compensation fee and postage; the clerk initials and date-stamps the top portion of the certificate and returns it to the sender. No special marking is required except for parcels containing fragile or perishable items.

Postal Orders

Postal orders are issued for 10p, and by multiples of $2\frac{1}{2}$p up to 25p; by multiples of 5p to £1 and by multiples of £1 up to £10. In addition to the face value a poundage is charged.

Up to $4\frac{1}{2}$p in postage stamps may be affixed on postal orders.

The sender of a postal order must enter in ink the name of the person to whom the amount is to be paid and is recommended also to fill in the name of the Post Office of payment. If the sender does not know the Post Office most convenient to the payee, he should write the name of the town, village or district where the payee resides and then it will be paid at any Post Office in the place named. (An illustration is given in Fig. 9.) A postal order may be crossed to ensure that payment is made only through a bank account. A counterfoil is attached and this should be completed, detached and kept for reference. If the sender has omitted to fill in the name of the payee, this must be done by the payee who must also sign his name on the postal order.

Fig. 9. A postal order
(*Reproduced by permission of the Post Office*)

Postal orders are valid for a period of six months from the last day of the month of issue. After the expiration of that period the order should be referred to the nearest Post Office or sent to the local head postmaster or, in London, to the district postmaster. If, after the necessary inquiry, payment is authorized, commission equal to the original poundage will be charged.

Telegraphic Money Orders

A money order for any sum up to £100 may be sent to the payee by telegraph. The issuing Post Office sends a telegram of advice to the paying office and a money-order telegram to the payee, who must take it to the Post Office named, sign his name and disclose to the clerk the name of the remitter.

The remitter must complete a requisition form with the names of the payee and remitter; the amount of money; and any message which may be required.

Cash on delivery

By means of the cash on delivery service, anything that conforms to the postal regulations for registered-letter post or inland-parcel post (up to a maximum of £100) may be sent to a firm's customer and delivered to him only on payment for the goods concerned. The money is collected by the postman, and the Post Office remits it to the sender.

The sender must write in ink on the cover of the packet:

a the name and address of the addressee;
b his own name and address;
c the amount of the trade charge, i.e. the amount to be collected from the addressee.

The sender must pay a C.O.D. fee, in addition to the normal postage and registration charges, calculated according to the value of the goods.

National Giro

The Post Office National Giro banking service provides a simple, cheap and fast means of transferring money. It operates through a single computerized organization, known as the Giro Centre, with an extensive network of Post Offices at which money can be paid in and withdrawn. Payment or transfer of money can be carried out either by using the mail service or by attendance at a Post Office. Instructions for payment or transfer are sent to the Giro Centre direct and not via the person or firm with whom the remitter is dealing. These instructions are processed by computer on the day they are received and statements of account and supporting documents are dispatched, also on the same day, thus providing a rapid 24-hour clearing service. Any person may pay money into a giro account at a Post Office by using an inpayment form, such as the one illustrated in Fig. 10.

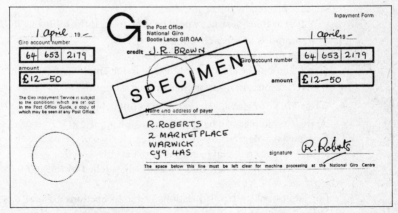

Fig. 10. A giro inpayment form
(*reproduced by permission of the Post Office*)

National Giro has the following advantages:
1 Post Offices are open for longer hours than banks.
2 The Giro Centre provides a 24-hour clearing service for transactions.
3 Regular statements with easy identification of items are sent to account holders.
4 No charges are made for transferring credit between account holders.
5 Paper work is reduced to the minimum as business documents such as invoices and orders may incorporate payment forms.

Questions

1 Write a letter to a friend explaining how she should prepare packages for registration.

2 If you wished to forward 79p to a friend, which Post Office service would you use and how would you deal with the matter?

3 What are telegraphic money orders? State the limit of amount, their advantages and the charges.

4 If you had to send banknotes by post, what method would you use to ensure their safety? Explain fully:
   a the steps you would take in packaging;
   b the Post Office service you would use;
   c the procedure you would follow at the Post Office;
   d the precautions the Post Office would take in order to ensure safe delivery of the package.   *(R.S.A.)*

5 Name three ways of sending money by post. Say in what circumstances you would choose each of them and explain the procedures necessary.   *(R.S.A.)*

6 Recorded delivery, registered post and compensation-fee parcel are three services offered by the Post Office.
   Which of these services would be used to send the following items:
   a a summons to appear in court;
   b a box of fragile glass samples weighing 5 lb;
   c a £5 note to be sent to the house of a sick employee?
   Give reasons for your answer in each case.   *(R.S.A.)*

7 Write True or False against each of the following statements:
   a Registered post can be used for transmitting £250.
   b A postal order to the value of £20 can be issued.
   c £75 can be collected by means of the C.O.D. service.
   d A telegraphic money order of £50 is dispatched by telegram   *(R.S.A.)*

For additional practical questions, refer to Sections 1.5 and 6.1 of *Practical Office Exercises*.

Unit 8 Duplicating processes

The principal methods of duplicating and copying business documents are:

1 Stencil   ⎫
2 Spirit   ⎬ producing *copies* of documents.
3 Offset-litho ⎭
4 Copying machine – producing *replicas* of documents.

Stencil process

A stencil, consisting of a sheet of special wax tissue, is 'cut' on a typewriter (or by hand) and is placed on an inked cylinder (see Fig. 11). Paper is fed into the machine which exerts the required amount of pressure to bring the ink through the perforations on to the paper as it passes between the cylinder and a roller. Semi-absorbent paper is normally used so that the ink is rapidly absorbed and there is no offset on the backs of the sheets of paper.

Handwriting is done with a stylus pen and a specially-prepared backing sheet, and photographs, drawings, forms, etc., can also be reproduced on a stencil duplicator if a special electronic scanner is used. These special stencils are prepared by the manufacturer or by the user, if he purchases the necessary equipment. There are hand- and electrically-operated duplicators, and thousands of copies can be obtained very quickly, particularly when an electric model is used.

Stencils can be filed away and used as and when further copies are required. They should be protected by semi-absorbent covers or placed in storage folders.

Colour work is not very conveniently done by the stencil process as a separate run is needed for each colour. The ink and the cylinder have to be changed and separate stencils used for each new colour, and care must be taken to see that each registers where it is intended to appear on the copy. An office with several duplicating machines could regularly use a different-coloured ink in each.

Fig. 11. A stencil duplicator (*reproduced by permission of Gestetner Ltd*)

Recommended uses of stencil duplicators

For 10 – 5000 typed documents for internal or external use; and the reproduction of large quantities of photographs, drawings and forms.

Spirit process

A 'master' copy is prepared by typing or writing on to a sheet of paper (half-art paper coated with china clay) backed by a transfer sheet coated with aniline dye. A mirror impression of the writing is made on the back of the master sheet, which is placed on the cylinder of the duplicator. The copy paper is moistened with spirit as it enters the machine and when it is pressed against the cylinder containing the master sheet, a positive copy is made. This process is very suitable for reproducing charts, drawings and other documents which require a variety of colours, as colour changes are made by using different-coloured transfer sheets in the preparation of the master copy. Handwriting and drawing on to the master sheet are done with a pencil or ball-point pen, and this is much easier than making the perforations required by the stencil process; drawings and diagrams can be prepared on special masters using a heat-transfer copying machine. There is a limit to the number of copies obtainable from one master sheet, as they tend to appear faint after some 200 to 300 copies have been duplicated. A spirit duplicator is illustrated in Fig. 12.

Fig. 12. A spirit duplicator
(*reproduced by permission of Nig-Banda Ltd*)

Recommended uses of spirit duplicators

For 10–250 copies of typed or handwritten documents for internal use; drawings, diagrams and all forms of commercial documents; and coloured work.

Offset-litho process

The 'master' for this process is a metal or paper plate, which is prepared by writing, drawing or typing through a litho ribbon, using special inks or photographic and electrostatic copying processes. The master sheet is fitted on to the cylinder of the duplicator and the printing ink is transferred from a roller to the master sheet before coming into contact with the copy paper as it passes through the machine. This process is very suitable for large quantities as a metal plate will produce 20 000 to 50 000 copies and a paper plate will produce about 2000 copies; it is commonly used by printers and also by many large offices. The work produced from an offset-litho duplicator is superior in appearance to that obtained by any other duplicating process, with photographs, drawings and the reproduction of colours among the impressive list of uses for which this process is eminently suitable. An offset-litho duplicator is illustrated in Fig. 13.

Fig. 13. An offset-litho duplicator
(*reproduced by permission of A. B. Dick & Co. Ltd*)

Recommended uses of offset-litho duplicators

For large quantities (100 – 50 000) of typed documents; the reproduction of large quantities of photographs, drawings and forms; coloured work; and sales leaflets, staff magazines, catalogues and price lists, and spare-part manuals.

Copying machines

A copying machine as illustrated in Fig. 14 enables the operator to produce an exact facsimile of any written, printed or drawn document;

it is quick and reliable because there is no possibility of any copying errors being made. The machines are electrically operated and the 'master' from which the copies are made does not have to be prepared in any special way. There is usually no limit to the number of copies which can be taken at any time but, if more than say ten copies are required, it is usually cheaper to use a stencil or spirit duplicator, but this depends on the type of copying equipment available.

Fig. 14. A photocopying machine
(*reproduced by permission of Nig-Banda Ltd*)

The main types of copying machines are:

1 Photocopiers using a wet process, e.g. transfer diffusion.
2 Heat transfer using a dry process.
3 Light transfer, a dry process, as in dual spectrum.
4 Electrostatic (xerography).
5 Dyeline using a wet chemical or vapour.

Recommended uses of copying machines

For 1–10 copies of a full-page printed document, extracts from books, photographs, diagrams and drawings; and copying legal documents, insurance policies, etc.

Safety precautions when using electrically-operated machines

1 Inspect the plug regularly.
2 Avoid having a trailing flex which may be a hazard for the operator or other staff passing by.
3 Always switch off the machine when it is not in use and remove the plug.
4 If the machine is not functioning properly, do not tamper with the electrical parts but call on the services of a mechanic.
5 Cover the machine when not in use to protect it from dust.

Working instructions

(a) Stencil duplicating

1 Remove carbon paper from a new stencil.
2 Anchor the head of the stencil on to the duplicator and then, turning the handle slowly with the left hand and holding the other end of the stencil with the right hand, allow the stencil to fall into position on the cylinder, smoothing out any creases as it revolves.
3 Tear off the backing sheet.
4 Select the most suitable size of duplicating paper, prepare it for duplicating by 'fanning' it to allow the air to separate the sheets, place it in the feed tray and raise the feed tray to the required position.
5 Pass the first sheet of paper through the machine and study it carefully. This first copy provides you with a clue to any further adjustments which may have to be made before beginning the run, e.g. more space at the top of the document or at one of the sides. Use the paper economically in these trial turns.
6 Make sure that there is sufficient ink in the machine.
7 Set the receiving tray so that the copies will fall naturally into it without buckling.
8 Set the automatic counter to the number of copies required.
9 Connect the electricity and switch on.

After the duplicating is finished:

10 Disconnect the electricity.
11 Take off the stencil by detaching it from the cylinder at the heading.
12 Remove surplus ink from the stencil by blotting it with absorbent paper, and place the stencil in a folder for storage.
13 Drop the feed tray.
14 Check that there is no paper still caught in the machine and replace all unused paper in its packet.

15 Leave the roller lever in the 'off' position.
16 Dust the machine so that paper fluff is eliminated.
17 Replace the dust cover.

(b) Spirit duplicating

1 A hand-written master is prepared by writing on the master sheet with
   a ball-point pen or sharp pencil and the hectographic transfer sheet is
   placed underneath with the carbonized surface facing upwards. It is
   preferable to use a backing sheet to provide a smooth surface, but only
   normal pressure should be used for writing.

2 For preparing a typewritten master the typist should use a normal touch
   and she should ensure that the type characters on her typewriter are
   perfectly clean. It is not necessary to disengage the ribbon for preparing
   spirit masters.

3 If an error is made, it is necessary to remove the carbon impression on
   the glossy side of the master. The following methods may be used:

   a A soft eraser (made specially for the purpose) will absorb the carbon
      and, at the same time, replace the original surface. Although it leaves
      a dirty mark, this will not show up on the copies.

   b A corrective fluid may be painted very thinly over the error and this
      replaces the clear china-clay backing.

   c A sharp instrument may be used to scrape away the carbon, but the
      disadvantage with this method is that it also scrapes away the china-
      clay backing.

   After the incorrect material has been removed, the correction should
   be made, and for this it is necessary to insert a piece of unused transfer
   sheet behind the master, so that the carbon content of the alteration
   will be the same as for the rest of the master.

4 On completion of the master, check it thoroughly with another typist.

5 Check that the spirit (fluid) level on the duplicator is not empty. The
   felt pad must be primed with fluid before running off the copies. In
   order to dampen the felt pad, move the fluid-control lever backwards
   and forwards several times.

6 To test that the felt pad is sufficiently damp for duplicating, set the
   pressure control at (1) and hand-feed one sheet of paper through the
   machine without inserting the master at this stage.

7 To hand-feed, the roller must be turned twice and the lever returned
   to the 'neutral' position. The dampness of the copy paper can be seen
   clearly, as the top of the paper remains dry.

8 Check that the feed tray is in line with the registration tray.

9   The master is fixed to the machine so that when the roller is turned, the carbonized surface is uppermost. Place the handle in the 'neutral' position, open the master clip, insert the master and finally close the master clip, which fixes the master to the roller.

10   Hand-feed one sheet of copy paper with the pressure at (1) to see if any adjustment is necessary to the height or depth of the master. An adjustment may be made by turning the registration-control wheel.

11   The copy paper should be thoroughly fanned to allow the air to separate the sheets.

12   Insert the paper into the machine, adjusting the side pads as required, and the right-hand paper guide is closed up to the side of the paper using the paper-guide release lever.

13   Drop the automatic feed wheels by hand and turn the knurl shaft until the paper curls a little.

14   Set the pressure control at (1) and fluid control at (1) and duplicate the number of copies required. For quantities of fifty or more the pressure control will have to be adjusted to higher numbers and the fluid control may need a higher setting depending on the density of the master.

15   The counting device should be set at '0' and this will then indicate the number of copies run off.

16   When the duplicating is finished, take the following action:

     a   Remove the master by releasing the master clip.
     b   Return the master clip to its closed position.
     c   Return the fluid control lever to '0'.
     d   Return the pressure control lever to '0'.
     e   Ensure that the handle is returned to the 'neutral' position.
     f   Replace the unused paper to its packet.
     g   Replace the dust cover, as this protects the duplicator from dust and damage.

Questions

1   State the most efficient manner of obtaining the following, taking into account economy of money and time:

     a   six additional copies of a closely typed foolscap sheet;
     b   fifty copies of a circular letter, for internal use, now in rough manuscript draft;
     c   as in *b* but 500 copies required;
     d   one thousand copies of a two-page typed document, which includes a diagram.   *(R.S.A.)*

2   You have been made responsible for a new duplicator, which is to be used by personnel from other departments. Draft instructions, in the form in which

they are to be displayed in the office, for the use and care of the duplicator.
(R.S.A.)

3 You are joining a new organization which has not yet fully equipped its office. You will be expected to send out monthly reports. What apparatus would you suggest should be bought:

  a if the number of copies is between 50 and 100;
  b if the number of copies is 5000 or more?   *(R.S.A.)*

4 What is the value of the photographic method of reproducing documents? What other methods of duplication do you know of?   *(R.S.A.)*

5 On what material would you type, and what ribbon would you use to produce media for the following processes:

  a spirit duplicating;
  b offset-lithography?   *(R.S.A.)*

6 Write notes on the preparation of a master for a spirit duplicator and the subsequent rolling off of 200 copies. Mention the advantages and disadvantages of this method of duplicating.   *(R.S.A.)*

7 Describe how you would prepare a rotary duplicator for the production of 500 copies of a letter, and say what precautions you would take to keep the machine in good running order.   *(R.S.A.)*

8 When would you use the following methods of copying letters and other documents:

  a photocopying;
  b carbon copying;
  c spirit duplicating;
  d ink duplicating?

  Give reasons for your choice.   *(R.S.A.)*

9 Two new duplicators, one ink and one spirit, are being installed in your office and supplies have to be ordered. Make a list of the supplies required for each duplicator and explain why each of the items relates to the one type of duplicator only.   *(R.S.A.)*

10 *a* Describe three ways in which a stencil can be prepared for ink duplicating.
   b Explain the limitations of each of the three ways described in *a* above.
                                                                        (R.S.A.)

11 In each of the four parts of this question, select the correct answer:

  (i) Where should you store the spirit used for spirit duplicating:

    a in a cool place;
    b in a corridor;
    c on a radiator;
    d near a naked flame?

(ii) The correct type of paper for use with an ink duplicator is:
    a absorbent;
    b positive;
    c spirit copy;
    d bank.

(iii) Hectographic carbon is used with:
    a a spirit duplicator;
    b a stencil duplicator;
    c an adding–listing machine;
    d NCR paper.

(iv) An electronic scanner is used to:
    a answer the telephone;
    b see inside an unopened letter;
    c prepare a stencil or offset-litho plate;
    d make a copy of a document.   *(R.S.A.)*

For additional questions, refer to Section 2.10 of *Practical Office Exercises.*

Unit 9 Filing

Office forms and correspondence are filed not only for purposes of preservation, but to have information contained in them available for quick reference. Requirements for filing differ; the firm with few correspondents does not require the elaborate system of the firm with many. The large variety of filing equipment which is now obtainable includes vertical-suspension cabinets, horizontal-plan cabinets, lateral installations, microfilm processes, etc., but whichever method is selected, it is important that the system used has the following essential qualities:

1 It must be quick and simple to operate.
2 The equipment must be compact and should not take up too much office space.
3 It must be capable of expansion or contraction.
4 The cabinets must be conveniently situated in the office and the files within the cabinets easy to locate.
5 The most suitable form of classification must be used to cater for the size, volume and nature of the correspondence to be filed.
6 Only 'live' correspondence should be held in the cabinet and 'dead' files, i.e. files no longer required, should be transferred to another cabinet which need not be kept in the office.

Methods of classification

The principal methods of classification are the following:

a alphabetical: correspondents' names
                    geographical
                    subject;
b numerical;
c combined alphabetical and numerical.

Alphabetical

In the alphabetical method each folder is given the name of a correspondent and the folders are arranged in strict alphabetical order. Guide cards, miscellaneous suspension files or individual letter bars are used

| Hill, P. L. & Co. |
| Heath, W. K. |
| Harrod's Television Service Co. |
| Hammond, K. |
| H   MISCELLANEOUS |
| Griffith & Barrett |
| Green, F. J. & Son |
| Godfrey, M. |
| Gilbert, Smith & Sons |
| Garner, T. W. |
| G   MISCELLANEOUS |
| Freeman Bros. |

Fig. 15. The alphabetical method of filing

to divide the letters of the alphabet. The first letters of the surname
determine the position of the file in the drawer. Fig. 15 illustrates the
alphabetical arrangement of files. Miscellaneous files are used for
holding small amounts of correspondence when individual files are
not needed. The front cover of a miscellaneous file should contain an
index of the names of the correspondents enclosed.

Geographical

In the geographical system the correspondence is classified according
to the place of each of the correspondents, i.e. country, county, town,
etc. The principle is identical to that of the alphabetical method, except
that papers are filed by alphabetically-arranged places instead of alphabetically-arranged correspondents' names. The correspondents' files
are, however, arranged after the appropriate place file. Fig. 16 is an
illustration of this method. The geographical system is used to group
papers and files in district or territorial order, e.g. in transport, export,
sales and planning offices.

Subject

In this method, papers are filed under the heading of subject matter.
This system is used for filing general correspondence which is not
concerned with specific individuals, such as letters relating to the
activities of a company, advertising, shipping, management, etc., where

Spencer, T.	
Liverpool	
Partridge & Dove	
Lincoln	
Johnson Bros.	
Leicester	
Pollock & Sons	
Leeds	
Watts, F. G.	
Browning & Sons	
Lancaster	
L	MISCELLANEOUS

Fig. 16. The geographical method of filing

it is convenient to have all the relevant data and correspondence concerned with any one topic grouped together for easy reference.

The primary guides in subject filing give the main headings of the subjects; for example, in the illustration given in Fig. 17 the subject primary guides are staff, stationery and typewriters.

Record cards	
Maintenance contract	
TYPEWRITERS	
T	MISCELLANEOUS
Quotations	
Orders	
STATIONERY	General
Salaries	
Outings	
Holidays	
Establishments	
STAFF	General

Fig. 17. The subject method of filing

Numerical

Files are arranged numerically, each correspondent being allotted a number. Index cards or index strips are required to connect the numbers with the names. Each index card contains the name of the correspondent and his allotted file number, and is arranged in alphabetical order in an index-card drawer. When a file is required, a number must first be obtained from the index card and then the appropriate file can be found in the filing cabinet. This method would be used for correspondence with a large number of clients or customers or for account records, particularly if coded and prepared by computer. It is capable of indefinite expansion as new files are placed at the back of existing ones. The number of the file is useful as a reference to be used on all relevant correspondence, and the index card or strip is useful for maintaining an address record or for making notes, e.g. when someone borrows a file.

An illustration of the numerical arrangement of files and an index card is given in Fig. 18.

Filing cabinet

| 460 |
| 459 |
| 458 |
| 457 |
| 456 |
| 455 |
| 454 |
| 453 |
| 452 |
| 451 |
| 450 |

456

CROW, P.,
11 Lander St.,
Boxley.
Monthly account

Index card

Fig. 18. The numerical method of filing

Combined alphabetical and numerical

The alphabetical system referred to above may also incorporate reference numbers, as illustrated in Fig. 19. Each letter or part of a letter is given a number, and a further number is allocated to each file as it is made; for example, if letter B is numbered 2 and there are twelve files in the B section, the last file to be opened is numbered 2/12. It should be noted that the files are arranged alphabetically and the numerical

C	MISCELLANEOUS	3
Burgess, J.		2/8
Bryant & Miller Ltd.		2/3
Brown, G. T.		2/5
British Motor Cycle Co.		2/9
Booth & Sons Ltd.		2/1
Black, A. I.		2/10
Bishops & Spears		2/2
Bennet, P. L.		2/6
Beard Bros.		2/7
Baxter Stores Ltd.		2/11
Barber, P.		2/4
B	MISCELLANEOUS	2
Avon Manufacturing Co.		1/6

Fig. 19. The alphabetical—numerical method of filing

aspect is secondary and is used as a reference number for correspondence.

The efficiency of a filing system depends not only upon using the most suitable equipment and method but on the ability and reliability of the filing clerk. The following rules are therefore necessary to ensure complete accuracy and easy access to all papers filed:

1 Correspondence should be filed daily so that the files are always up to date.
2 The papers should be placed in the files in the correct sequence of dates so that the most recent document is on top.
3 Large bulky files should be avoided, and correspondence which is not currently required should be separated from the current file and placed into a 'dead' file. A reference to the number of the 'dead' file should appear on the current file.
4 Individual papers should not be removed from a file in the filing cabinet. If an individual paper *must* be removed, a note stating the date, name of correspondent and the name of the person holding the paper should be placed in the file.
5 If a file is temporarily removed for reference, an 'absent' marker or card should be completed.

Fig. 20. A vertical filing cabinet (*reproduced by permission of Abbott Bros Ltd*)

6 When there is insufficient correspondence on one subject or with one correspondent to justify opening an individual file, a 'miscellaneous' file should be used.
7 Adequate cross-references of file titles should be made either on the file covers or on index cards.
8 Filing must always be carried out methodically and neatly.

Filing equipment

Vertical filing cabinet

In this method the files are arranged vertically (upright) and papers can be inserted or replaced without removing the file (see Fig. 20). The titles appear on the top edges and can be read easily. The files may be sus-

Fig. 21. A lateral filing cabinet (*reproduced by permission of Roneo Vickers Ltd*)

pended vertically from metal runners fitted inside the cabinet drawers which protect them from wear and tear.

A disadvantage of using the vertical method is the amount of space required not only for the cabinet itself but for opening the drawers.

Lateral filing cabinet

The files are stored side by side in a lateral filing cabinet and the titles are placed vertically along the front of the files (see Fig. 21). Space does not have to be allowed for the opening of drawers and the cabinets can be built up as high as the ceiling will allow. A large number of files can be on view at the same time, but because of the large opening they may attract dust. A disadvantage of this method is the difficulty experienced in reading the titles arranged vertically, but this can be overcome by using a numerical system.

Plan filing

Plans and drawings may be stored horizontally in flat drawers or vertically in storage cabinets where the drawings are arranged in an upright position. Fig. 22 illustrates a vertical plan file which contains compartments with wave-like dividers enabling large drawings to stand erect without buckling. A vertical cabinet occupies less than a third of the

Fig. 22. A plan filing cabinet
(*reproduced by permission of Roneo Vickers Ltd*)

floor space of a horizontal cabinet of equal capacity. Each compartment has its own indexing strip so that the drawings can be easily identified.

Microfilming

This is a method which is used to reduce the space occupied by business documents and correspondence. The papers are photographed and when reference is required the film is fitted into a viewer where the documents can be seen in enlarged form. It saves space and is an efficient method of storing the information required in a large organization. Fig. 23 shows a section of microfilm.

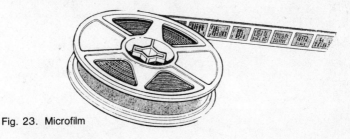

Fig. 23. Microfilm

Questions

1 Draw up simple rules for a new employee who, under your supervision, will deal with the filing of correspondence.

2 What do you consider to be the essentials of a first-class filing system?

3 When opening a new filing system, what would influence you in your choice between alphabetical, numerical, geographical or subject methods of indexing?

4 Distinguish between numerical and alphabetical filing systems. When would you advise the use of the numerical system?   *(R.S.A.)*

5 Why is a card index necessary with numerical filing? Draw up two sample cards and fill in the details. When would you use this system of filing?   *(R.S.A.)*

6 You are responsible for filing all letters and documents in a small firm. State the essentials you would look for in your filing system. Give your reasons.
                                                                          (R.S.A.)

7 Which method of filing would you use for the sales departments of the following:

   a a small cutlery business;
   b a large concern with 1000 credit customers;
   c an exporting firm, with agents in many overseas countries.

   Give reasons for your choice.   *(R.S.A.)*

8   Outline the procedure to be taken by a filing clerk when:

    a   a paper may be correctly filed under more than one letter of the alphabet;

    b   a member of another department wishes to take out a file.   *(R.S.A.)*

9   *a*   What is lateral filing? Draw a diagram to help illustrate your explanation.

    b   What are the principal advantages of lateral filing?   *(R.S.A.)*

10   Select the correct answer below:

    An index card is necessary for the location of file names in a:

    a   geographical system;

    b   numerical system;

    c   subject system;

    d   alphabetical (name) system.

Indexing

The first finger is generally used for pointing and is called the index finger. An index is something which points to the place where certain information may be found. In business, where time is generally considered to be very precious, indexing is understood to be the arranging of the names of correspondents, customers or others with a view to facilitating reference to letters, accounts, orders, etc. Of course it includes the arranging of any names or details at the beginning or end of a book, in a separate volume or on cards, so that the information may be used for reference. Indexes are drawn up alphabetically in surname order, although it is obviously better to use the permanent name of a firm rather than the names of its officials. Both may be taken if it is thought desirable; for example, a letter to Henry Sharp, Secretary, Wigfield Coal Co. Ltd, is indexed under W; it may also be indexed under S for Sharp. Titles, such as Mr, Esq., Messrs, are omitted.

The card index

A card index consists of a tray, box or drawer in which cards containing the required information, plainly written or preferably typewritten, are arranged alphabetically and, if necessary, secured by a rod which passes through a hole or slit in the cards. To prevent the cards from falling flat, an adjustable or sliding block at the back is moved forwards. Guide cards with projecting parts are arranged at the required intervals and, if necessary, tab cards with smaller projections are used for further classification. Metal or plastic signals or indicators may also be used, and the colours of the guide cards may be varied to aid selection. The record cards may be cross-referenced, and they may serve several purposes, e.g. giving addresses, ledger folios, letter-file numbers, particulars of credit, quotations, etc. Both sides of the card can be used if necessary.

Visible-card systems

Visible-card and strip-indexing systems can be employed for a large number of office and shop-record purposes such as staff records, sales records, accounts, mailing lists, current retail prices, stock records, etc. The information in the records can be seen at a glance as the cards or strips are arranged so that the titles are all visible. The exposed portions carry, in addition to their titles, various control features which summarize essential details contained in entries on the records. Colour markers or indicators can be clipped to the cards for identification purposes. Transparent plastic shields are generally fitted over the exposed portions of the cards to protect them from dirt and to provide a suitable carrier for the coloured markers. An illustration of a visible-card system is given in Fig. 24.

In a system of strip indexing each item of information is recorded on a separate strip, and these are then built up one above the other in suitable carrying devices, so that all the information contained in them

Fig. 24. A visible-card record system
(*reproduced by permission of Roneo Vickers Ltd*)

is exposed to view. Additions, amendments and deletions can be made without affecting the continuity of the records. The strips may be housed in panels, wall fitments, books, stands, revolving units or cabinets. Individual reference to addresses, telephone numbers, prices, quantities or measurements, each on its own strip, can be made easily and information pin-pointed quickly.

Rules for indexing

When arranging files or index cards in alphabetical order, the filing clerk should observe the following rules:

1 The surname is placed before the Christian names and, if the surnames are the same, the first Christian name determines the position, e.g. Williams, Henry would be placed before Williams, Robert.
2 If the Christian name and surname are embodied in the name of a firm, the surname is written first, followed by the Christian name and finally by the remainder of the name, e.g. John Smith and Co. Ltd would be filed under Smith, John, and Co. Ltd.
3 When 'The' is the first word of the name, it is either omitted or placed at the end, e.g. Perfect Trading Co., The.
4 If a firm has several names, the first name is taken as the surname for filing and indexing purposes, e.g. Messrs Light, Brown and Jennings, should be filed under 'Light'.
5 The first name is used in hyphenated names, e.g. in Banks-Price use 'Banks'.
6 Names beginning with Mac, Mc or M' are treated as if they were spelt 'Mac'.
7 Titles are placed after the surname and before the Christian name, e.g. Titmus, Sir Peter.
8 Names beginning with St are treated as if they were spelt 'Saint'.
9 Nothing comes before something, i.e. a name without an initial precedes a name with an initial, as in the following names: Parsons; Parsons, A.; Parsons, A. A.
10 Names which consist of initials are placed before full names, e.g. P & O Lines Ltd precedes Pollard & Co. Ltd.

Office memory aids

Office memory aids designed to keep appointments, meetings and current business matters (following up letters) under review include:

1 Office Diary – the simplest of the aids and one of the most effective methods provided that it is systematically maintained and referred to daily.

2 Indexed Memory Aids – in which index cards or memorandums are used to record the matters which require attention on future dates. The system consists of folders for each day of the month and each month of the year which are stored in a filing cabinet. When a matter requiring attention on a future date arises or when appointments are made, an entry is made on a card or memo and placed in the appropriate file. The folders are then referred to every day, and after a day's entries have been dealt with, that file is placed at the back of the month's files.

3 Signalling Devices – using different colours for each month on visible record cards, as explained earlier in this unit, to highlight the date when a matter on the card requires attention, e.g.

1	2	3	4	5	6	7	8	9	10	11	12	13	14	15	16	17	18	19	20	21	22	23	24	25	26	27	28	29	30	31
1	2	3	4	5	6	7	8	9	10	11	12	13	14	15	16	17	18	19	20	21	22	23	24	25	26	27	28	29	30	31
1	2	3	4	5	6	7	8	9	10	11	12	13	14	15	16	17	18	19	20	21	22	23	24	25	26	27	28	29	30	31

Questions

1 Prepare the kind of index card a school would use for its students, and explain how use could be made of coloured cards and signalling devices.

2 Discuss the uses and advantages of visible-card and strip-indexing systems. Place the following names of individuals, professional bodies and trading organizations in the order and form in which you would index them:

Rowland Denbigh   The Dental Supply Company
Robert Denby   Dennis Howard and Brothers Limited
Denmore and Jones   De Rosa Nurseries
Jones and Denmore   *Design Weekly*
The Dennison Lamp Company Ltd   O'Donovan and Sons
Lord Denman   Derry O'Donovan
Derby Ex-Service Club   De La Rue and Company Limited
                                                        (R.S.A.)

3 *a* Under which letters of the alphabet would you file:

(i) James Brown & Sons;
(ii) James, Brown & Sons;
(iii) Parker-Smith Industries;
(iv) O'Maherty Supplies Company;
(v) Peter St John Associates?

b Explain the rules to be followed when filing alphabetically names beginning with Mc and Mac, e.g. McIntosh, MacAlister.   *(R.S.A.)*

4 Arrange the following in the order in which you would expect to find them in an alphabetical filing system:

Mrs R. Van Whynke   Mrs P. V. C. Heath
Miss B. Quick   Price & Prattle, Solicitors
Robert E. Heath, Esq.   The Southern Box Company of Essex
The City of Westminster   M. G. Gibb, M.D., B.Ch.   *(R.S.A.)*

5 Make a list of *three* memory aids in general office use and then write a paragraph on each one you have chosen, describing how it is used in practice.

6 Draw up simple rules for an office junior who is responsible for indexing files of correspondence.

7 *a* List the following names in alphabetical order for filing or indexing purposes:

F. Fisher & Sons   Dr H. N. Skelton
Secretarial Services   Law Accident Insurance Society Ltd
The City of Sheffield   J. M. Renshaw
Department of Employment   I. Skellington
  and Productivity   Stewart & Lloyds
The Metal Box Co. Ltd

b If you were in charge of a centralized filing system, what would you do to ensure that papers taken from files could always be traced and returned to their correct places?   *(R.S.A.)*

8 Select the correct answer below:

The name ST JOHN AND RED CROSS DEPOT would be indexed alphabetically under the letter:

a D;
b J;
c R;
d S;

For additional practical questions, refer to Sections 2.6 and 2.7 of *Practical Office Exercises.*

Section B:
Business communications

The principal methods of communication in business are the following:

1 Letters and memos.
2 Telegrams and teleprinters.
3 Telephone.

Other methods of communication commonly used in business include:

1 Intercom.
2 Pocket paging.
3 Loudspeaker (tannoy).
4 Closed-circuit television.
5 Reports/circulation slips.
6 Meetings/conversation.
7 Notice boards.

The choice of which method of communication to use depends on several factors, e.g. the urgency, length, safety and secrecy of the message, whether a written record is required and a consideration of the cost involved.

The units in this section of the book give the essential factors which have to be considered by the office junior when she is preparing and presenting any of the principal forms of communication. She must also learn to select the most appropriate method and, when she writes a letter, makes a telephone call or sends a telegram, she must ensure that the message is clear, accurate and businesslike.

Unit 11 Business letters

The writer of a business letter should always aim at being accurate, clear, brief and courteous.

Accuracy is attained by the cultivation of the habit of careful reading and careful checking, especially of figures, dates and prices, and also by the correct use of words.

Clearness is attained when the sender and receiver naturally get the same meaning from the words. An example will demonstrate the kind of difficulty which may arise: if, say, on Monday, 'next Thursday' is mentioned in a letter, it may be taken by some people to mean the Thursday of the following week, and by others to mean the Thursday of the current week.

Business correspondents should avoid using more words than are strictly necessary to express the meaning clearly and courteously. In the following examples the words in italics are not necessary to the sense: '*entire* monopoly'; 'We supply only *pure and* unadulterated oil'; 'We must decline *to accept* your offer'. Excellent practice for attaining brevity is afforded by summarizing, in which the aim is to seize the chief ideas and express them briefly.

A letter must be set out clearly and correctly. The numbers set out in Fig. 25 relate to the following points:

1. Date
The date must be typed in the order of the day, month and year, as 11 June 19 . . .

2. Reference
The reference on a letter may consist of the initials of the dictator and the typist, such as Our Ref PFC/JH, or it may consist of the file reference number, such as Our Ref 1427. The reference of the addressee should always be used whenever it is known.

3. Inside name and address
This is the name and address of the addressee and it should be accom-

modated in three or four lines if possible. The postcode should appear immediately below the postal town.

Messrs Pemberton and Sons
162 Regent Street
LAMPTON
SN7 2PX

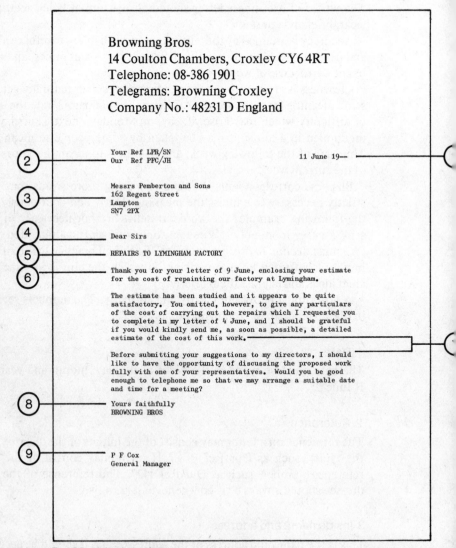

Browning Bros.
14 Coulton Chambers, Croxley CY6 4RT
Telephone: 08-386 1901
Telegrams: Browning Croxley
Company No.: 48231 D England

② ─── Your Ref LPR/SN
Our Ref PFC/JH   11 June 19—

③ ─── Messrs Pemberton and Sons
162 Regent Street
Lampton
SN7 2PX

④ ─── Dear Sirs

⑤ ─── REPAIRS TO LYMINGHAM FACTORY

⑥ ─── Thank you for your letter of 9 June, enclosing your estimate for the cost of repainting our factory at Lymingham.

The estimate has been studied and it appears to be quite satisfactory. You omitted, however, to give any particulars of the cost of carrying out the repairs which I requested you to complete in my letter of 4 June, and I should be grateful if you would kindly send me, as soon as possible, a detailed estimate of the cost of this work.

Before submitting your suggestions to my directors, I should like to have the opportunity of discussing the proposed work fully with one of your representatives. Would you be good enough to telephone me so that we may arrange a suitable date and time for a meeting?

⑧ ─── Yours faithfully
BROWNING BROS

⑨ ─── P F Cox
General Manager

Fig. 25. A business letter

4. Salutation

This is the writer's greeting. It is governed by the relationship which exists between those corresponding and the usual salutations for business correspondence are Dear Sir(s) or Dear Mr Hunt.

5. Heading

If there is a subject heading as in Fig. 25, it should stand out clearly. It should be noted that there is no full stop at the end of a heading.

6. Opening sentence

This is used to introduce the subject matter of the letter by referring to the previous letter, telephone conversation or telegram or, if there has been no previous correspondence, by referring directly to the subject matter.

7. Body of letter

The sentences and paragraphs in the body of a letter must be arranged so that they appear in logical sequence and so that each aspect of the subject is dealt with in a separate paragraph.

8. Subscription (or complimentary close)

This is the closing complimentary remark in a letter, and it is again governed by the relationship existing between those corresponding and by the salutation already employed. The usual subscriptions for business correspondence are: Yours faithfully, with Dear Sir(s); and Yours sincerely, with Dear Mr Hunt.

9. Description of signatory

In a business letter the name of the business is usually typed immediately under the subscription and the name of the writer and his position in the business are typed five lines below this, as in the following example:

Yours faithfully
CHAMPION INVESTMENTS LTD

G. H. Champion
Managing Director

Memorandum forms

Memos are used for internal communication or for messages or reports to agents in other parts of the country or the world. The salutation and subscription are dispensed with and the heading normally contains the writer's name or position, the name or position of the addressee, the date and the file reference.

Circulation slips and envelopes

Circulation slips and envelopes are used for internal circulation of correspondence and journals to members of staff. A circulation envelope is illustrated in Fig. 26.

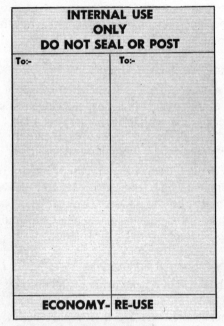

Fig. 26. A circulation envelope

Questions

1 Write a letter from Messrs Merchent & Co., of Market Street, Stafford SD8 4AL to Rylands & Sons Limited, Wood Street, London EC4 3AX enclosing a cheque, value £42.85, in settlement of the January account, requesting delivery of the balance of an order made on 29 March, and (for stock-taking purposes) asking for a statement up to the end of March to be forwarded by 7 April.

2 Rewrite this letter in better style:

Dear Sir

Thank you for your communication of 10 inst, which came to hand today. The aforesaid letter is receiving our prompt attention, but we respectfully beg to point out that owing to a recent strike we are unable to deal with same within this week. Assuring you of our best attention at all times and trusting that you will continue to favour us with your esteemed orders.

Yours faithfully, *(R.S.A.)*

3 Write a letter expanding the following notes:

Goods damaged, probably through careless packing. Useless. Await instructions. Must have sound goods.

4 *a* When would you use the word Messrs, and when omit it?

b When would you use Esq. in preference to Mr?

c If you sign a letter E. Johnson, how will you indicate that you are a woman and unmarried?

d When would you use: (i) Yours faithfully, (ii) Yours sincerely? *(R.S.A.)*

5 What do you understand by 'internal memorandums'? Give an example and state their advantages. *(R.S.A.)*

6 Using an accepted layout, write a reply to the following advertisement:

Junior Clerk required for Medical Records Department at the Liverpool Royal Eye Hospital, Main Street, Liverpool 1. Salary £550 per annum at age 16 and £650 per annum at age 17, rising to a maximum of £900 per annum. Preference given to candidates who have passed the 'O' Level GCE Examination in at least three subjects.

Applications, giving full details of age, education, qualifications, previous experience (if any) and the names of two referees (one of whom should be a previous employer or head teacher), should reach the Secretary by 15 June 19...

(R.S.A.)

7 On your way to the office you are involved in an accident which results in an injury to your knee. Write (in proper form) a letter to your employer, explaining the reason for your absence from work. Rule and address the envelope.

(R.S.A.)

8 *a* What is the difference between a memorandum and a circulation slip?

b State three other methods of passing a message between departments.

(R.S.A.)

9 Which of the following is *not* a method of communication:

a telephone;

b telex;

c letter;

d *P.O. Guide*?

For additional practical questions, refer to Sections 2.1, 2.2 and 2.3 of *Practical Office Exercises*.

Unit 12   Stationery and equipment for the typist

The typist is expected to keep her typewriter and the other items of equipment which she uses in good condition to enable her to produce work of a high standard and quality.

In order to keep her typewriter in good condition she should:

1 Have the typewriter serviced regularly by a mechanic.
2 Dust and clean the machine regularly.
3 Brush the type with a stiff brush every morning.
4 Cover the machine at night, and whenever it is not in use.
5 Use a backing sheet when using a single sheet of paper in order to protect the platen and improve the appearance of the typewriting.
6 Move the carriage fully to the left or right when erasing to avoid the eraser dust dropping into the type basket and clogging up the keys.
7 When moving the typewriter, lift it by the base from the back and lock the carriage in the centre position by bringing the margin stops together.

Electric typewriters

Electric typewriters are being used more and more in offices today. They enable typists to type with very little physical effort and they can therefore type quickly for much longer periods than are possible on manual machines. Many more carbon copies can be taken at one time and the electrically-controlled impression provides a sharp, even striking of the keys which is ideal for the preparation of duplicator masters and stencils. One electric typewriter, known as the IBM golf-ball typewriter, has dispensed with type bars and uses a small cylindrical head which contains all the usual characters. When the keys are operated the typing head revolves to the character required – the carriage does not move (see Fig. 27).

Special-purpose typewriters

Typewriters which are designed to produce work for special purposes include:

Fig. 27. A cylindrical head (golf ball) for the IBM Typewriter (*reproduced by permission of IBM (United Kingdom) Ltd*)

Typewriter	*Purpose*
1 Card-holding attachment	To enable stiff cards, such as index cards, to be fed into a typewriter and curved around the cylinder.
2 Continuous stationery	For typing forms which are fed into the typewriter in continuous form. The carbon paper stays in position making it unnecessary for each set of forms to be interleaved with carbons.
3 Dual unit (containing two type units)	For typing scientific and mathematical formulae when narration and formulae characters are mixed.
4 Flexowriter	For automatic typing from punched tape which is suitable for preparing letters and documents where the same information has to be reproduced several times. It is also used for preparing data for transmission by teleprinter or telephone.
5 Front-feed device	To enable invoices or other documents to be inserted from the front of the typewriter, while the journal sheet is held in the machine by the normal feed roller.
6 Hectograph carbon roll	For typing master sheets for use on spirit duplicators.
7 Justowriter	For automatic typing with justified margins.

Typewriter	*Purpose*
8 Magnetic tape/card	For automatic typing. It records on magnetic tape or card the matter typed and if corrections are necessary these are made by typing over the incorrect material.
9 Varityper	For producing typewriting with justified margins which looks like printers' type. It contains interchangeable type styles and sizes.

Dictating machines

Dictating machines use either a magnetic or a non-magnetic media (see Fig. 28).

Magnetic dictating machines do not provide a permanent record, and corrections are made by the dictator simply talking on top of the incorrect passage. The tapes, sheets, etc., can be used indefinitely as new recordings take the place of previously-dictated material.

A permanent record can, however, be made on the non-magnetic dictating machines, and there is no danger of the recording being cleared before it has been transcribed by the typist. Corrections have to be noted by the dictator on an indicator slip, or dictated at the end of the passage, and it is then the responsibility of the typist to see that the alterations are made at the correct points in the dictation. An

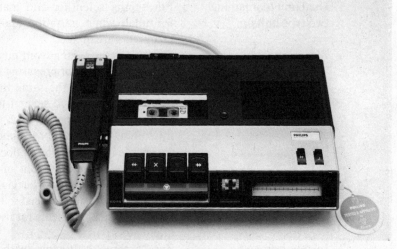

Fig. 28. A dictating machine
(*reproduced by permission of Philips Electrical Ltd*)

advantage of the non-magnetic medium is that the dictator and typist can see clearly the amount of dictation recorded.

The typist who types from a dictating machine is known as an audio-typist. The following list of hints are important for efficient transcription from a dictating machine:

1 Note any special instructions and corrections accompanying the record.
2 Assess the size of each letter before typing it to enable the correct size of paper to be used.
3 Urgent letters should be typed, checked and delivered to the dictator first of all.
4 Check any doubtful points in the dictation with the dictator or supervisor.
5 Use a dictionary for looking up the spelling of a word whenever you are in doubt.
6 Insert the correct punctuation marks and allow adequate new paragraphs.
7 Letters must be carefully checked before they are removed from the typewriter.
8 Switch off the electric power whenever your dictating machine is not in use and cover the machine.

The materials used for recording media include tape, plastic belts, plastic discs, plastic or paper sheets and wire. Tapes are sometimes provided in a specially-designed plastic case, known as a cassette, which is simply slotted on to the machine making it unnecessary for the tape to be threaded on to the spool.

The main advantages of using a dictating machine are that the dictator can dictate matter when his typist is not available, such as during the luncheon interval or in the evening and the typist can be employed on other work whilst the dictation is being given.

However, any doubtful points do not come to light until later and, because the typist has not previously listened to the dictation, it is more difficult for her to correct grammatical points and assess the new paragraphs.

Carbon paper

In order to produce good carbon copies and prevent creasing, the typist should:

1 Keep the carbon paper in a flat box.
2 Be careful when fitting the carbon paper into the machine as, at this stage, careless handling will cause it to crease.
3 If the paper and carbon paper feed unevenly, ascertain whether the feed-roll mechanism on the typewriter requires adjustment.
4 Keep the box of carbon papers away from a hot radiator or from the sun. NCR (no carbon required) paper may be used for forms such as invoices as an alternative to using carbon paper and carbon-backed paper. The reverse side of the top copy and the top sides of the sheets below are specially treated with chemicals to allow copies to be made without carbon paper. When an impression is made on the top copy it causes the chemically-treated surfaces of the paper to reproduce the impressions on the copies beneath.

Typewriting Paper

Types of paper

a Bond – a good-quality type of paper which is used for headed paper and 'top-copy' work.
b Bank paper (or flimsy) – a cheaper and lighter grade of paper used for carbon copies and sets of forms.
c Duplicating paper – semi-absorbent paper used for stencil duplicating or non-absorbent paper used for spirit and offset-litho duplicating.
d Airmail paper – very thin (lightweight) paper for correspondence sent by airmail.

Paper sizes (international measurements)

A3 = 297 mm x 420 mm – used for balance sheets, large legal documents, etc. ($11\frac{3}{4}$ in x $16\frac{1}{2}$ in)
A4 = 210 mm x 297 mm – the most commonly used size for business correspondence ($8\frac{1}{4}$ in x $11\frac{3}{4}$ in)
A5 = 148 mm x 210 mm – used for small letters ($5\frac{7}{8}$ in x $8\frac{1}{4}$ in)

Paper quantities

Quire = 24 sheets – used for stencils, carbons, etc.
Ream = 480 sheets – used for paper.

Envelopes

1 Banker envelopes – the opening is on the longer side.

2 Pocket envelopes – the opening is on the shorter side.
   The international measurements for envelopes include:
   C6 = 114 mm x 162 mm
   D1 = 110 mm x 220 mm

3 Window envelopes – contain a 'window' opening with transparent material, dispensing with the need for the typist to type the name and address on the envelope.
4 Aperture envelopes – as (3) but with an uncovered panel.

Post-Office preferred envelopes (POP)

At a future date, envelopes outside the Post-Office preferred range of sizes may be liable to an additional charge. They must be at least 90 mm x 140 mm and not more than 120 mm x 235 mm.

Questions

1 When large numbers of invoices are sent out regularly they are often typed on paper which does not have to be separately inserted in the machine.
   a What is this paper called?
   b How is it used?
   c What are the advantages? (R.S.A.)

2 The typewriter is perhaps the machine most commonly found in offices today. Mention the kinds of work for which it can be used. Give *three* essential precautions to be taken if it is to provide good service. (R.S.A.)

3 Say what you know about the use of recording machines in offices. Mention any advantages and/or disadvantages. (R.S.A.)

4 Mention *three* common sizes of office stationery, and say for what purposes each is used. (R.S.A.)

5 The following terms refer to office stationery:
   bond, bank, flimsy, absorbent.
   a What do you understand by them?
   b For what purposes would you use each of these types of stationery? (R.S.A.)

6 Make a list of four qualities which an audio-typist should possess. (R.S.A.)

7 What equipment would you use for (*a*) fastening papers together, and (*b*) preparing papers for insertion in a looseleaf binder? (R.S.A.)

8 *a* Name the container in which a tape is held in position on some dictating machines.
   b Name recording media other than tape. (R.S.A.)

9 *a* Name three kinds (not makes) of typewriters.
   b State some advantages of each.
   c For what kinds of work would you use them? Give reasons. (R.S.A.)

10 *a* What are 'window' or 'aperture' envelopes and when are they used? Mention their advantages and disadvantages.

    b What happens if:

      (i) A letter is understamped;

      (ii) A letter contains no stamp;

      (iii) There is no reply when a postman brings a registered letter. *(R.S.A.)*

11 Describe each of the following, using diagrams where helpful:

    a banker envelope   a pocket envelope

    a window envelope   a business-reply envelope *(R.S.A.)*

12 Automatic typewriters are very different from manual and electric typewriters. Explain this statement and in your answer refer to some of the uses made of automatic typewriters in offices today. *(R.S.A.)*

13 *a* To remain efficient, an office typewriter needs to be well cared for. Suggest three ways in which a typist can, in her daily use of the machine, take care of her typewriter.

    b What are the advantages of an electric typewriter? *(R.S.A.)*

14 *a* Your office junior frequently asks for fresh supplies of carbon paper. What advice would you give her on the use and care of it?

    b What is NCR paper? *(R.S.A.)*

15 *a* List the essential features, other than the subject content, of a business letter.

    b Name the two international sizes of paper most widely used in business offices, and give one example of the work for which you would use each size. *(R.S.A.)*

16 In each of the three parts of this question, select the correct answer:

    (i) A ream of paper contains approximately:

       a   240 sheets;

       b   1000 sheets;

       c   100 sheets;

       d   480 sheets.

    (ii) NCR paper should be used:

       a   to make a negative for dye-line copying;

       b   to make simultaneous copies of a document without using carbon paper;

       c   as copy paper for ink duplicating;

       d   as copy paper for spirit duplicating.

    (iii) Semi-absorbent paper should be used for:

       a   taking carbon copies on a typewriter;

       b   producing copies on a spirit duplicator;

       c   producing copies on an ink duplicator;

       d   taking copies in a receipt book. *(R.S.A.)*

Unit 13 Addressing envelopes

When addressing envelopes, the typist should pay attention to the following requirements:

1 The name and address must be displayed correctly.
2 The correct form of address must be used.
3 The correct postal address must be given.

The envelope address must contain:

a The name of the addressee.
b The number of the house or flat and the name of the street.
c The name of the village or district.
d The name of the postal town in block letters. Postal addresses are given in the book *Post Offices in the United Kingdom* or, for local addresses, reference can be made to the local telephone directory.
e The name of the county in which the postal town is situated (except for addresses in London and certain other large towns, and where the name of the town is the same as that of the county, e.g. Warwick, Warwickshire would be an unnecessary duplication). An example is given in Fig. 29.
f The postcode which should occupy the last line of the address.

```
    For the attention of Mr J Penn

    Messrs Brown Jacobs & Sons
    421 Cranbury Road
    EASTLEIGH
    Hants
    SO5 5HT
```

Fig. 29. An envelope

The name and address should be displayed in the following manner:

1 The name should be written or typed in the centre of the envelope and it should commence half-way down.
2 Each item of the address should start on a separate line.
3 The name of the postal town should be written in block capitals.
4 'Private', 'Confidential' or 'For the attention of . . .' are usually typed two spaces above the name.

Forms of Address

The student should ensure that the correct forms of address are used by referring, whenever she is in doubt, to *Titles and Forms of Address* by Black.

Individuals

W J Smith Esq. or Mr W J Smith.

(Use either 'Mr' or 'Esq' but never use both. The typist must use whichever form her employer prefers.)

When the abbreviations 'Sen' (Senior) or 'Jun' (Junior) are included in the name, they should be placed immediately after the surname.

Mr James Johnson Jun.

Mr Peter Johnson Sen.

Use the husband's Christian name when addressing a married lady, e.g. Mrs Peter Johnson.

If, however, the lady is a widow, her own Christian name should be used, e.g. Mrs Rosemary Packwood.

Two unmarried ladies should be addressed 'The Misses', e.g. The Misses Pamela and Margaret Parker.

A partnership

The title 'Messrs' should be used for a partnership, except when the name of the firm is preceded by the word 'The' or a title; for example:

Messrs Brown Collins & Company
The Precision Tool Company
Sir Thomas Williams & Sons

A limited company

The title 'Messrs' should not be used for a limited company because the communication is addressed to the company and not to the members referred to in the name. It should be noted that a limited company is an incorporated body, i.e. *one* legal person, and the word 'Messrs' meaning several men should not be used. For example:

> James Brown & Co. Ltd
> or
> The Sales Manager
> James Brown & Co. Ltd

French names

Monsieur Edouard Dupre.

(The abbreviations, M = Monsieur and MM = Messieurs, are not used when addressing envelopes or in the salutation of a letter. They may be used in the text of a letter when referring to a third person.)

A firm: Eduard Dupre et Cie.

German names

An
    Herrn Max Muller

A firm: An
            Petters G.M.B.H.

(The name of the town is usually written immediately under the name of the person or firm, followed by the street.)

Dutch names

De Heer M Wilderychx (Mr is also frequently used.)

A firm: Myne Heren Wilderychx u Goris

(The street number is written *after* the name of the street.)

Spanish names

Sr Dan G Fernandez

A firm: Srer S y J Ramirez
            Mudarra e Hijos

Italian names

Sig P Rossi

A firm: Ditta Engico

Belgian names

As for French or Dutch names.

Addressing Machines

Addressing machines may be used for addressing envelopes for circulars and also for writing names and addresses on invoices, statements, wage slips and packets and other business documents. The information is placed on a 'master' stencil or plate and, when this is passed through the machine, the address is transferred on to the envelope or document very much more quickly than would be possible by handwriting or typewriting and the operation is carried out with absolute accuracy. It is estimated that 100 envelopes can be addressed in 4–5 minutes by using an addressing machine, compared with over 40 minutes when using a typewriter.

Questions

1 Write the following addresses as you would do on envelopes intended to go by post:
John Thompson 14 Eden St Wakefield WD6 7AR
Clarkson & Jackson Cotton Spinners Heald Road Blackburn BN4 3OR
Finlayson Bros Virginia St Glasgow GW1 3AL
Secretary Midland Hardware Company Ltd Church Street Stafford SD1 4AS
K Percival Manager of the Midland Bank Ltd Colmore Row Birmingham 14S 3AG
A W Brooks Junior Bow Chambers 37 Moorgate London EC2 4AS

2 What special precautions should be taken in the addressing of envelopes?

3 When should the title 'Messrs' be used in the address on an envelope?

4 Which part of an address on an envelope should be typed in capital letters? Why is this?

5 Correct any of the following forms of address which you consider to be wrong:
    a   Messrs Bright Tools Limited;
    b   Johnson James & Sons;
    c   J. Spencer Sen. Esq.;
    d   L. M. Arnott B.Sc. Esq.;
    e   Miss Joan Wood and Miss Mary Wood;
    f   Brown Jones & Co. Ltd;
    g   Major T. K. Watts Esq.

6 a   Place the following in the correct form and order for indexing purposes:
        R. M. MacDonald
        Peter Smith-Ryland
        The International Rubber Co. Ltd
        District Council of Winchester
        McDougall Bros

Mace and Morgan
South Midlands Construction Co. Ltd
James Webb & Co. Ltd
Sir Ian Spencer & Sons
Royal Air Force High Wycombe
Major R. L. Webber
Rector of St Mary's Church Stanforth: Rev. P. L. Stubbs
Jeremy Smithers MP for West Banktown
James de la Rue

b In a separate list show the names with the appropriate titles where necessary for addressing envelopes, e.g. Messrs, Esq. etc.   *(R.S.A.)*

7   What are the main uses of:
a   a varityper;
b   an addressing machine?   *(R.S.A.)*

8   Select the correct answer below:
An addressing machine is used for:

a   opening envelopes;
b   franking envelopes;
c   pre-listing invoices;
d   addressing invoices.   *(R.S.A.)*

Unit 14 Telegrams and teleprinter services

In this unit we shall discuss the part played by the telegram and teleprinter services as a reliable and rapid means of business communication.

Telegrams

The telegram service provides a quick method of sending urgent written messages to all parts of the country, although with the greater use of telex, telegrams are not used so much in business. The message can either be written on a form which is handed over the counter at a Post Office or it can be dictated over the telephone or sent to the Post Office by telex.

The charge for a telegram is calculated on the number of words used and so it is important to exclude all unnecessary statements. The chief points to be considered in the drafting of a telegram are:

1 Clearness must never be sacrificed in order to reduce the cost.
2 Grammatical completeness of sentences may be ignored.
3 The essential figures should be written in words.
4 Avoid using slurred words, such as can't, won't, don't, etc.
5 The name and address of the addressee should not be abbreviated unless a telegraphic address is known.

Telegram forms

Telegram forms should be written or typed in block capitals and handed over the counter of a Post Office. A duplicate copy of the message must be retained for the file and on the day of dispatch a letter of confirmation should be sent to the addressee. The name and address of the sender should be written on the back of the telegram form as well as the name of the sender appearing on the front of the message. The example of a telegram given in Fig. 30 answers the following question:

Send a telegram from Messrs Horlake and Brett, 45 Albany Street, London W1 3AB to Messrs Calder and Wimborne, 12 New Square,

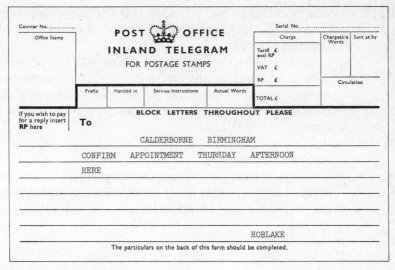

Fig. 30. A telegram form
(*reproduced by permission of the Post Office*)

Birmingham 14S 3AP stating that Horlake and Brett can arrange for the interview to take place at their address at 1500 hrs on Thursday of this week, as suggested in Calder and Wimborne's last letter.

Telegraphic address

In the example only two words are used for the addressee's name and address. This is a registered telegraphic address. Such an abbreviation is possible on payment of an annual fee and registration of the name at the Post Office. A telegraphic address is used by businesses who receive or send a large number of telegrams.

Telephoning telegrams

Even if a message is being telephoned, it is advisable to draft out the text and record it on a message form in much the same way as if the telegram were being sent from a Post Office counter. A copy of the message is then available for filing and a note can be made on the copy of the date and time the telegram was sent.

A telegram can be dictated at any time from a private telephone or from a public telephone kiosk. To obtain the telegraph office a caller should dial the code given in the telephone directory. When the operator answers 'Telegrams', the exchange and number from which the caller is speaking should be given and the message dictated clearly, two or three words at a time. When the Post Office operator reads back the message, it should be checked very carefully with the copy of the telegram dictated.

A telexed telegram should be prepared in a similar manner. After connecting the telex line to the Post Office telegrams number, the message has to be typed on the teleprinter. This provides a more reliable method of dispatch as the telegram is reproduced in written form at the Post Office.

An overnight telegram

An overnight telegram is one which is handed in to a Post Office between 0800 and 2230 hours for delivery the following morning or the next postal delivery. The charge is less than that for an ordinary telegram.

Prepaid-reply telegrams

A reply to an inland telegram may be prepaid by the sender up to a limit of £3.50. A reply-telegram form showing on the back the amount prepaid will be delivered with the telegram to the addressee. When a reply-paid telegram is delivered by telephone, and a reply is not dictated at once, the reply form is posted with the confirmatory copy of the telegram. The addressee may use the reply form in payment or part-payment for a telegram or a telephone account rendered by the Post Office.

Cancellation of telegrams

A telegram may be cancelled by the sender after it has been accepted for transmission. If the request for cancellation is made before transmission has begun, the charges paid, less a small fee, are refunded. If the message has already been transmitted, an official telegram is sent to the delivery office and the normal charge is made. If the cancellation telegram does not overtake the original before delivery, the sender is informed.

Teleprinter services

A teleprinter, as in Fig. 31, is an instrument for sending and receiving urgent written messages in code form over a telegraph or a telephone line. Private telegraph facilities may be rented from the Post Office or a person or business may rent a line in the Post Office telex system.

The telex system provides a very quick means of written communication by teleprinters among subscribers. It combines the speed of the telephone with the authority of the written word. A printed copy of the message is available at both the sending and receiving teleprinters. Calls can be made to any telex subscriber in the United Kingdom and to subscribers in a large number of overseas countries, including the USA. The service is available day and night and messages may be transmitted to a subscriber even though his teleprinter is unattended, provided it is switched on. Inland and overseas telegrams can also be sent from a telex teleprinter to a Post Office telegraph office or to Cable and Wireless Telegraph offices for onward transmission at normal telegram rates, and incoming telegrams can be accepted directly on to the teleprinter.

There is a standard rental charge for the provision of the necessary equipment and for hiring the line to the telex exchange. Charges for the calls vary according to the distance between the calling and called subscribers' telex centres; details are given in the *Post Office Guide*.

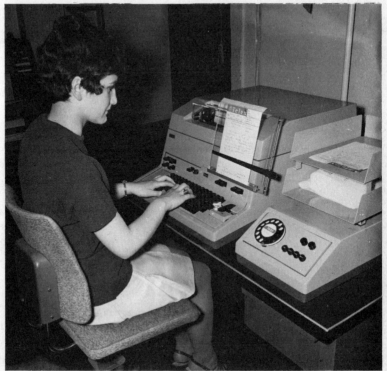

Fig. 31. A telex teleprinter (*reproduced by permission of the Post Office*)

The procedure for operating a telex teleprinter is:

1 The operator dials the correspondent's telex number (obtainable from the United Kingdom Telex Directory).
2 Correspondent's answerback code (an abbreviated name) must appear on the teleprinter before any further action can be taken.
3 The operator types her own answerback code.
4 The operator types the message.
5 The operator repeats her answerback code.
6 Correspondent's answerback code must appear on the teleprinter again to confirm that the full message had been transmitted.

The uses of telex are:

1 It provides an instant written communication which is ideal for many business purposes.
2 It is a reliable means of communication for messages of a technical or quantitative nature.
3 Foreign languages can be translated more easily in the written form provided by telex.
4 It can be used to receive messages when the office is closed, which is particularly useful for communications from overseas.
5 Telegrams can be received and dispatched by telex.
6 It can be used for transmission of computer data by the Datel Services.

Questions

1 Make out a telegram from Messrs Sharp & Co., to Messrs Field & Sons, Leek, stating that the remittance promised by Field & Sons has not arrived; the goods ready for delivery cannot be forwarded until their cheque for the amount of the invoice has been received.

2 Make out a message to be sent by telegram from Messrs Marchant & Co., of Leicester, informing Smith & Co. Ltd, Market Street, Cambridge that, owing to an unexpected rise in the market prices, quotations given last week will not hold good, and that an advance of 5 per cent will have to be made on the prices submitted.

3 List three advantages that the telex system has over the telephone.   *(R.S.A.)*

4 *a* Why is the telegram now so seldom used in business?
   b Give two alternative methods of sending urgent messages and briefly state your reasons for your choice.   *(R.S.A.)*

5 State two methods by which inland telegrams can be sent using Post Office facilities, and describe the steps to be taken when using these.   *(R.S.A.)*

6 Prepare the following message for transmission by telegram to XL Engineering Co. Ltd, 24 Palmerston House, Cannon Street, London EC4 3AX:

Please send an engineer to repair our packing machine No XTP 4473 in which one of the arms has jammed. This is the fifth time during the past year that the machine has gone wrong and work is repeatedly held up in the Despatch Department. Unless you can ensure that these continual stoppages cease, we shall be compelled to discontinue our contract with you.

You are sending the telegram from Summers Confectionery Ltd, 221 Harwich Avenue, Ipswich IH4 8SO.   *(R.S.A.)*

7 What is the telex service? For what purposes is it generally used? Mention its advantages and disadvantages (if any).

8 Pair the following words, e.g. if you consider that *a* in the first column pairs with *c* in the second column, write *c* against *a*:

a telegram	*a* answerback code
b telex	*b* telegraphic address
c telephone	*c* duplicating
d electronic scanner	*d* STD

For additional practical questions, refer to Section 2.5 of *Practical Office Exercises.*

Unit 15 The telephone

The business student should acquire the ability to answer the telephone confidently and efficiently; this can be obtained chiefly from practice and a thorough knowledge of telephone services and technique. Answering the telephone is an important duty because the office junior is representing her firm and the tone of her greeting and the manner in which she handles the call will create in the caller a favourable or unfavourable first impression.

It costs nothing and is very little more trouble to extend a pleasant, helpful and courteous greeting to all callers and, in return, it will enhance the company's reputation and help to make its business dealings friendly and cordial. The following instructions suggest ways in which the telephonist can acquire skill in handling telephone calls:

1 Answer the telephone quickly and be as concise as possible.
2 Announce the name of your firm, e.g. 'Williams, Smithers and Company'. On no account should you waste the caller's time by saying 'Hello'.
3 Speak slowly and distinctly in a conversational tone, avoiding slang expressions, such as 'Hang on', 'Right-ho', etc.
4 Do not repeat matters overheard on the telephone.
5 Learn the names, positions held and activities of all who use the telephone in your organization so that you can connect callers quickly to the right persons.
6 If the person required is not available, ask the caller whether he wishes to leave a message, be rung back, ring again later or speak to someone else. Whatever action is taken you should note the caller's name, business address and telephone number.
7 If an incoming call is disconnected, you should replace your telephone receiver and the caller will re-establish the call as soon as possible. If, on the other hand, you are making the call and it is disconnected, then you should signal the Post Office operator by flashing the telephone bar or operating a switch on the switchboard to have the call reconnected, or dial the number again if using an automatic exchange.
8 When a call is being transferred from one extension to another, you should convey the caller's request to the new extension so that he is not

inconvenienced by having to repeat his request more than once. If a delay occurs before the caller can be connected, keep him informed of the action you are taking.

9 When you receive a call which is a wrong number, you should remember that the intrusion is probably no fault of the caller and that if the caller apologizes, you should accept it politely. If, on the other hand, you are put through to a wrong number, you should offer an apology as the mistake is certainly not the responsibility of the person called.

10 Private calls should not be made except in special cases of urgency.

11 Most of this country is now served by STD (Subscriber trunk dialling), in which 'GRACE' (Group routing and charging equipment) takes the place of the Post Office telephone operator. This equipment interprets the instructions dialled by the caller, directs the call to its destination and, when it is answered, automatically records the number of units used on the caller's meter. Brevity on the telephone is, therefore, essential with STD as every unit of time is recorded. STD operates on the basis of 1.8p units which buy varying amounts of time according to the distance of the call, the day of the week and the time of the day.

Telephone numbers are gradually being changed to all-figure numbers; the exchange name is replaced by figures which include the STD code. For example, the telephone number of Sir Isaac Pitman and Sons Ltd, in London is 01-242 1655. The figures before the hyphen are the STD code and those after the hyphen form the local number.

Intercom

An intercom (see Fig. 32) or an internal telephone system is used for internal communication between departments. Alternatively, internal telephone calls may be made on the Post Office telephone when it is part of a PABX system, as explained below.

Switchboards

A switchboard is essential in an office when there are several extensions in order to receive and route the incoming calls to the required extensions.

PMBX — an abbreviation for private manual-branch exchange — is a system in which the telephonist makes all the connections between the extension users within the firm and the incoming and outgoing calls.

PABX — an abbreviation for private automatic-branch exchange — is a system in which extension users are able to dial their own external

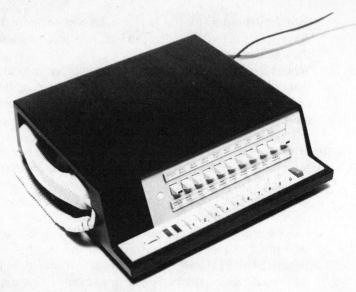

Fig. 32. A push-button intercom
(*reproduced by permission of Shipton Automation Ltd*)

calls without using the services of the switchboard operator; they can also dial one another which provides a means of internal communications in the one telephone. The switchboard operator must, however, be used to receive and route incoming calls.

Post Office telephone services

Several of the most important telephone services provided by the Post Office are described below. Full information and current charges for these services are set out in the *Post Office Guide*.

Personal-call system

A personal telephone call is one in which the caller specifies the name or reference of the person to whom he wishes to speak, and is offered by the Post Office for the payment of a small extra charge. The charge becomes payable as soon as an inquiry has been made at any distant number quoted by the caller, whether the call has been effective or not, but only one fee is payable irrespective of the number of attempts made to complete the call. The timing of a call does not start until the connection has been made to the person required. If he or acceptable substitutes cannot be traced, only the personal fee is payable.

A personal call enables a caller to:

1 Quote the name of the person to whom he wishes to speak, the names of any acceptable substitutes and the telephone numbers where all or any of them may be found.
2 Specify the person to whom he wishes to speak by a reference code, title or department, or by an extension number.
3 Arrange to speak only if two named persons are both available at one particular number.
4 Arrange for a person not on the telephone to be brought to a neighbour's telephone, whose number he gives.

If the personal call cannot be completed at once, the originating exchange operator will leave a message at the distant telephone asking the wanted person to ring the personal-call operator at the calling exchange as soon as possible. Alternatively, either the caller or the person answering at the called number may give the time at which further attempts should be made to obtain the person wanted or quote another number at which he may be found.

Fixed-time calls

A trunk call may be booked in advance to be connected at or about a specified time if the lines are available. A small extra charge is made for this service.

Transferred-charge calls

A charge for a telephone call may be transferred to the called subscriber, if he agrees to accept it. A request for this must be made at the time the call is booked and an additional small fee is payable.

Time service

The telephonist can obtain the correct time by making a call to the speaking-clock service which is operated in London and certain other centres. All announcements of the time are given from the clock at intervals of ten seconds. In areas in which this service is unobtainable, the telephonist can obtain the time as given by the local-exchange clock by asking the exchange operator. The fee payable for these services is that for an ordinary local call.

Directory enquiries

Enquiries about telephone numbers are answered free of charge by all telephone exchanges. The telephonist must dial the number for 'Directory Enquiries'.

Advice of duration and charge (ADC)

The cost and duration of a telephone call made via the operator will be notified on its completion for an additional small fee, provided the operator is asked for this service at the time of requesting the call.

Telephone credit cards

Travellers or representatives may use a telephone credit card to enable them to make telephone calls and send telegrams from any telephone without payment at the time. A credit card bearing a serial number is issued to each person using the service and when a telephone call is made the caller must quote his serial number to the operator. Credit-card holders are required to obtain calls through the operator and cannot dial direct. Calls on credit cards are charged to the telephone account on which the card was issued, and are either listed separately or distinguished by a letter or number on the account. The normal charge plus a small fee is made for the credit calls and for each credit card there is a quarterly charge.

Freefone

Another service which allows people to use the telephone without charge to themselves is Freefone. If a firm wishes to encourage people to telephone them it can apply to the Post Office for a special 'freefone' telephone number. By using this number the firm's customers or clients are entitled to telephone them without charge. It encourages customers to place orders by telephone and it can also be used by representatives and employees to save them the time and trouble of using coins and claiming refunds from their firms. The basic charge is related to the area served by the firm. In addition, the firm is required to pay the normal telephone-call charge plus a transferred-charge call fee for each 'freefone' call. All such calls must be accepted without question.

Telephone-answering machine

If it is necessary to provide a 24-hour-a-day telephone service to an organization, which may be necessary in the case of firms receiving communications from all over the world, such as service engineers in television or news agencies, an answering machine may be connected to the telephone. A telephone-answering machine gives a pre-recorded announcement inviting the caller to record a message. The messages are recorded on magnetic tape, which are then transcribed and typed on to message sheets the following morning or whenever the staff return to the office. This device provides a continuous telephone answering and recording service and it is particularly useful for using at lunch time and when the organization closes down for the night.

Overseas telephone calls

Subscribers with STD can dial direct to numbers on exchanges on the Continent and in some other countries. Calls via the operator are controlled at the International Exchange which should be obtained by dialling the relevant codes.

Questions

1 Draw up a set of rules for the efficient use of the telephone to guide junior clerks who have recently joined your office.

2 Describe the Post Office telephone services which can be used for:
   a booking a telephone call in advance;
   b finding the time of day;
   c making an inquiry about a person's telephone number which is not in the local directory.

3 If your employer wished to speak personally to Sir Brian Phillips, who is Managing Director of Phillips Machine Tool Company, Manchester, how would you arrange this for him?

4 What advice would you give to a new junior clerk about receiving and making private telephone calls during office hours?

5 What do you understand by the following terms:
   a STD;
   b Fixed-time calls?   *(R.S.A.)*

6 *a* Mention one kind of information (other than the time) you can obtain automatically through the telephone.
   b If you lift the receiver to answer an incoming call and hear a series of rapid pips, what does this indicate?
   c What should be your first words when answering a telephone call?
                                                                          (R.S.A.)

7 *a* What is the cost to a subscriber of an STD unit of time?
   b On what does the length of time in an STD unit depend?   *(R.S.A.)*

8 What do you understand by the following terms:
   a Directory enquiries;
   b Transferred charge calls?   *(R.S.A.)*

9 *a* What should a junior do to ensure that she deals intelligently with an incoming telephone call?
   b Some firms forbid personal calls for their employees. Why do you think this is done?
   c Why do people sometimes make 'Personal' calls? What is the procedure?
                                                                          (R.S.A.)

10   Name three of the special telephone services provided by the Post Office which give, by dialling particular codes, immediate information on certain matters or events.   *(R.S.A.)*

11   Letters, internal memoranda, telex, telephone, are all methods of communication. When would you use each of them?   *(R.S.A.)*

12   *a* Explain the personal-call telephone service provided by the Post Office.
     b Name two publications issued by the Post Office for telephone users.
     c Explain the advantages of the freefone service.   *(R.S.A.)*

13   Explain the following details featured on a company's headed notepaper:

452 2233 (STD Code 061)

Telex 23721

Cables MANCUNIAN STOCKPORT

In what circumstances would you use these methods of communication?
                                                                      (R.S.A.)

14   *a* What is the meaning of the letters STD?
     b How is the cost of such a call calculated?
     c How does this cost compare with the cost of calls connected by the operator?
                                                                      (R.S.A.)

15   In each of the three parts of this question, select the correct answer:
     (i)   STD is an abbreviation for:
          a Subscriber Telephone Directory;
          b Standard Trunk Dialling;
          c Subscriber Trunk Dialling;
          d Standard Telephone Directory.

     (ii) For immediate contact between departments large firms may use:
          a an automatic typewriter;
          b a dictating machine;
          c a telephone-answering machine;
          d an intercom.

     (iii) Which of the following is *not* an information service provided by the Post Office:
          a the speaking clock;
          b train departures;
          c road conditions for motorists;
          d weather forecasts?

Section C: Business forms

The business student should be familiar with the chief business forms used in the various departments of the organization by which she is employed, and in this section a description and illustration is given of the forms commonly used. There are, of course, many variations in the style and structure of these forms and the illustrations given here can only serve as a general guide. The student is reminded that in each industry and even in each business the forms which are used are modified to meet the particular needs of the kind of business carried on.

The chart overleaf shows, under the headings of the offices in which they are handled, the forms dealt with in this section. The arrows indicate the direction in which the forms flow through the various sections.

Mailing Office	Sales Office	Works Office	Buying Office	Accounts Office	Cashier's Office	Wages Office
Incoming Goods						
Price list						
Order						
Advice note						
Invoice						
Statement						
Cheque						
Outgoing Goods						
Price list						
Order						
Delivery note						
Invoice						
Statement						
Cheque						
Goods Returned Inwards						
Credit note						
Goods Returned Outwards						
Credit note						
Wages						

Goods Received note

Cheque

Statement

Credit note

Time cards
Tax deduction cards
Wages sheets

Wage packets

Unit 16 Ascertaining price and ordering goods

In this unit we shall discuss the various business forms which are required for the purpose of ascertaining price and ordering goods.

Ascertaining price

There are several ways in which the buyer can ascertain the price of the goods he wishes to purchase. He may, for instance, receive one of the following documents from the seller:

1 *A catalogue.* This usually consists of a printed pamphlet giving a description of goods offered for sale; catalogues are normally illustrated with photographs or drawings. Instead of including prices in their catalogues suppliers frequently decide to issue separate price lists. The catalogue and price list do not constitute a definite promise to sell as the goods are offered subject to stocks being available at the time the order is received.

2 *A price list.* This contains a short description and the current price of goods offered for sale; illustrations are not normally given in price lists. Fig. 33 is an extract from a price list which, on issue, gave the prices at which the firm was prepared to sell its filing cabinets.

3 *A prices current.* A price list must not be confused with a prices current, which contains lists of prices which may fluctuate from day to day with the state of the market. The prices current must always be marked with the date of issue and there are two principal ways of issuing one:

    a It may be issued weekly or monthly, in which case the buyer knows that the prices contained in the current list hold good until he receives the next prices current.

    b It may give the highest and lowest market price and in this case the buyer uses it to assess the approximate prices of goods offered for sale. Suppliers who use this method are under no obligation to sell goods at the prices quoted, but they will conduct their business at or near to these, depending on the state of the market.

4 *A quotation.* If the buyer is not in possession of catalogues and price lists, he will usually write a letter of inquiry to the supplier asking

AMALGAMATED ENGINEERS LIMITED MILLTOWN

RETAIL PRICE LIST

Standard range   colours | Olive Green or Grey with Anodized Aluminium Hardware

When ordering please state colour required

FILING CABINETS

Model	Description	Height	Price
			£
141	Double capacity with lock		16.65
141	Double capacity non locking	130 cm	16.05
142	Standard with lock		16.30
142	Standard non-locking		15.85
131	Standard with lock	109 cm	14.96
121	Standard with lock	64 cm	12.52
111	Standard with lock	45 cm	8.20

Note: All prices exclude V.A.T.

All cabinets are supplied with Compressors or Rails for suspended Filing. When ordering please state which is required. Measurements are 60 cm deep overall, Double Capacity 44 cm wide, Standard 40 cm wide; height as shown above.

Fig. 33. A price list

him to quote a price for supplying certain goods. The supplier then replies in the form of a quotation. This may be incorporated in the letter of reply or it may be set out on a special quotation form giving full particulars and conditions of sale. Occasionally a *pro forma* invoice (see page 107) is used instead of a quotation.

5 *An estimate.* Catalogues, price lists, prices current and quotations are issued for goods supplied at the standard dimensions and prices but,

where goods have to be supplied to a special pattern or where modifications have to be carried out, the supplier has to calculate the cost in accordance with the additional work entailed and an estimate is used to inform the buyer of the special prices involved.

6 *A firm offer.* If the seller decides to give the prospective buyer a special price for his goods, he writes a letter containing a firm offer. This offer is usually only open to the buyer for a certain period of time.

7 *A tender.* If a local authority or other public body requires goods or services to be supplied, it will ask for tenders to be submitted by a certain date. The tender is another method of offering to supply goods or to carry out work at a specific price and is similar to an estimate.

The literature, forms and letters giving details and prices of goods offered for sale are carefully filed in the buying office for quick reference at any time.

Requisition

A request to draw goods from stock or to purchase goods is made on a requisition form, as in Fig. 34. A stock requisition is used for requesting goods from stock and a purchase requisition is used when goods have to be bought.

PURCHASE REQUISITION			No: 123
Department: Sales		Section: Export	
Supplier's Name (if known): J. Barnwell & Sons			
Address: 52 Stringer Place, Bankston BN4 3AX			
Estimate Reference Number: S 18973		Capital/~~Revenue~~	
Signature of Head of Department: ~~Rubra~~.		Date: 1 October 19–	
Quantity	Details	Cat. No.	Price each £
6	Swivel armchairs in moquette	60M	14.25

Fig. 34. A purchase requisition

Fig. 35. An order form

The order

The order form is used by the buyer to obtain goods. The completed order illustrated in Fig. 35 is being sent to **Amalgamated Engineers Limited** for four filing cabinets, details of which are given in the price list on page 96.

Note the following items of information which should always be given on the order form:

1 Name and address of the buyer.
2 Name and address of the seller.
3 Serial number of the order (all orders issued should have a serial number so that this number can be quoted on future correspondence and on documents relating to the order).
4 Date of issue.
5 The quantity, description (including the model or catalogue numbers) and price of the goods.
6 Delivery instructions, i.e. the address to which the goods are to be delivered.
7 Signature of the buyer.

Office routine for purchasing goods

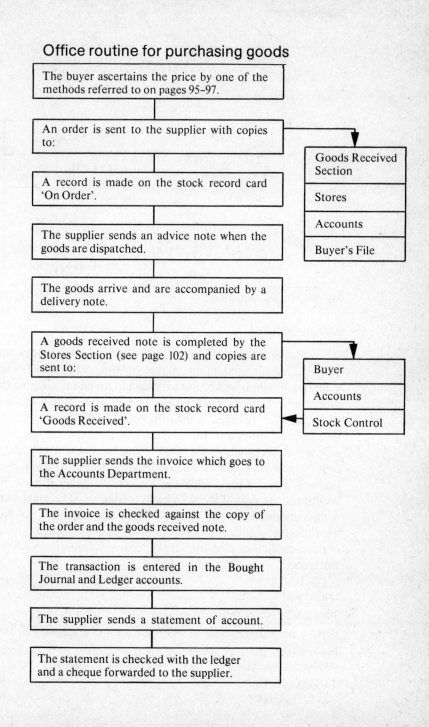

The buyer ascertains the price by one of the methods referred to on pages 95–97.

An order is sent to the supplier with copies to:

- Goods Received Section
- Stores
- Accounts
- Buyer's File

A record is made on the stock record card 'On Order'.

The supplier sends an advice note when the goods are dispatched.

The goods arrive and are accompanied by a delivery note.

A goods received note is completed by the Stores Section (see page 102) and copies are sent to:

- Buyer
- Accounts
- Stock Control

A record is made on the stock record card 'Goods Received'.

The supplier sends the invoice which goes to the Accounts Department.

The invoice is checked against the copy of the order and the goods received note.

The transaction is entered in the Bought Journal and Ledger accounts.

The supplier sends a statement of account.

The statement is checked with the ledger and a cheque forwarded to the supplier.

Stock card							
Item Type 105X						Max. Stock: 30	
Diesel Engines Mark II						Min. Stock: 10	

	RECEIPTS			ISSUES			BALANCE IN STOCK
Date	Quantity Received	Invoice No.	Supplier	Quantity Issued	Reqn. No.	Dept.	
1.1.19–							24
2.2.19–				12	121	Works	12
13.2.19–	15	A.126	Marks Ltd.				27
13.3.19–				6	129	Spares	21

Fig. 36. A stock-record card

Stock control

It is essential for the parts or materials ordered to be in stock when they are required for production. A stock-record card (or bin card as it is sometimes called) will be kept for each item and it will give the maximum and minimum stock figures (see Fig. 36). When the amount of stock has been reduced to the minimum figure the stock clerk knows that he must order a further quantity of the item. He is guided in the amount of his order, as the total of the balance in stock and the new order must not exceed the maximum stock figure. The minimum stock figure is set at a level which will allow the buyer time to replenish before the amount of stock in hand is used up. The maximum figure is also important as this should ensure that capital is not tied up in unnecessary stock, that valuable store-room space is not used unnecessarily and that the stock does not deteriorate whilst in the storeroom.

Questions

1 State the difference between a price list and a prices current.

2 Explain the different ways in which the price of goods may be ascertained.

3 Prepare (*a*) a purchase requisition and (*b*) an order form for obtaining the following filing cabinets quoted in the price list on page 96.

Two Filing Cabinets . . . . Model 142

One Filing Cabinet . . . . Model 131

4   Design a price list for a firm supplying record-players.

5   You are employed as a typist in the Order Department of a large manufacturing concern. Much of your work consists in typing orders. Explain what is involved in this work and give a brief account of the working of the department.

(R.S.A.)

6   What system would you suggest for the recording of orders received? Outline the procedure which follows their receipt.   *(R.S.A.)*

7   The firm you work for – Blackburn, Robson and Coates, of 29 Moor Road, Huddersfield HD7 4AX – has received an inquiry from W. Jessop, 178 Tufnell Street, Nottingham NM4 2OS about the following goods:

> 10 rolls men's suiting of good quality, in brown, grey and navy blue fine checks.
> 8 rolls tweed in heather mixtures.
> 12 rolls terylene and worsted suiting.
> All materials should be 130 cm wide. Delivery required in good time for autumn trade.

Draft and complete the document that would be sent by your firm in answer to this enquiry, giving all the essential information.   *(R.S.A.)*

8   You are responsible for the ordering and issuing of stationery in your department. What precautions would you take to ensure (*a*) that you do not keep too large a stock, and (*b*) that the stock does not run out? Give a sample of a ruling for the Stationery Stock Book.   *(R.S.A.)*

9   Select the correct answer below:

A document requesting the purchase of goods is called:

a   a purchase order;
b   a quotation;
c   a purchase requisition;
d   an estimate.

For additional practical questions, refer to Sections 3.1, 3.2 and 3.3 of *Practical Office Exercises*.

Unit **17** The receipt and dispatch of goods

The documents connected with the receipt and dispatch of goods are advice notes, goods-received notes and delivery notes.

Advice note

When goods are ready to be dispatched, the seller completes an advice note and sends it, usually at the second-class postage rate, to the buyer, informing him that the goods are on the way. The advice note gives details of the goods sent and the method of transport being used. On receipt of this, the buyer can prepare to receive the goods. This document is not usually prepared separately but is a carbon copy of the invoice with the omission of the prices.

Goods-received note

On arrival, the goods are checked against the advice note, and a goods-received note is prepared by a clerk in the Works office. One copy is retained for reference and duplicate copies are sent to the Buying and Accounts offices. The Buyer checks the details of the goods-received note against his copy of the order and the Accounts Clerk checks it against the invoice received from the supplier; if there is no error, the invoice is authorized for payment. A goods-received note contains the following details:

1 Serial number.
2 Name of supplier.
3 Date goods were received.
4 Quantity and description of goods received.
5 Order number.
6 Signature of the person who examined the documents against the goods received.
7 Signature of the person who received the goods.
8 Method of transport.

DELIVERY NOTE

J. BARNWELL & SONS
52 Stringer Place
Bankston BN4 3AX
Phone 07-384 1243

Commercial Stationers & Office Furnishers

Delivered to   Messrs. Woodman & Sons,
                 14 High Street,
                 Barchester,
                 BR8 4TY

Date 14th October, 197 .   Your Order No AT/189

	Please receive:	
SIX	Swivel armchairs in moquette Cat. No. 60M	Two crates
	Received in good order and condition by	

Fig. 37. A delivery note

Delivery Note

If the goods are delivered in the seller's van or lorry, the driver is given two copies of a delivery note: one is given to the buyer, and the other is signed by the recipient of the goods and returned by the driver to the seller. The packages should be carefully checked before the delivery note is signed. A delivery note, a specimen of which is given in Fig. 37, should contain:

1 Name and address of the seller (consignor).
2 Name and address of the buyer (consignee).
3 Serial number.
4 Date issued.
5 Order number.
6 Quantity and description of the goods and the number of crates, cartons, boxes, etc. in which the goods are supplied.

The delivery note is similar to the advice note and is usually prepared at the same time as the invoice.

Questions

1 Write a description of the documents handled in connection with the receipt and dispatch of goods.

2 Prepare an advice note for consignment of 200 shirts dispatched by rail.

3 For what purpose is a goods-received note issued? Who issues it and to whom are copies sent?

4 Complete a delivery note for the goods contained in the order on page 98 of Unit 16.

5 Select the correct answer below:

A goods-received note is completed when:

a goods are checked against the advice note;
b goods are ordered;
c goods are ready to be dispatched;
d goods are invoiced.

For additional practical questions, refer to Section 3.4 of *Practical Office Exercises.*

Unit 18 Invoices and credit notes

The business forms which are necessary for the recording of sales of goods or services, and corrections or returns, are invoices and credit notes.

The Invoice

Invoices are statements sent by sellers to buyers, giving particulars of goods sold. They are necessary when goods are purchased on credit, i.e. to be paid for in the future, and advantageous even with cash purchases. The particulars contained in an invoice vary, but the chief items include:

1 Name, address, telephone number, telex number and VAT registration number of the supplier.
2 Name and address of the buyer.
3 Serial number and date of the invoice.
4 Order number.
5 Terms of payment.
6 Quantity, price and description of the goods.
7 Trade discount.
8 Carriage and method of delivery.
9 VAT, if applicable.
10 Date of dispatch.

These items are shown in the specimen invoice illustrated in Fig. 38.

Before invoices are dispatched the greatest care must be taken to secure accuracy in all their details. They will usually be sent to the buyer by the second-class postage rate and they may also serve, in addition, as advice notes, notifying the buyer that the goods are on the way; they should not be sent in the parcel together with the goods.

On receipt, invoices should be checked against the copies of the orders and also with the goods. To ensure that checking is done, a rubber stamp is often used and, after carrying out the necessary work, the responsible clerk initials the blank spaces.

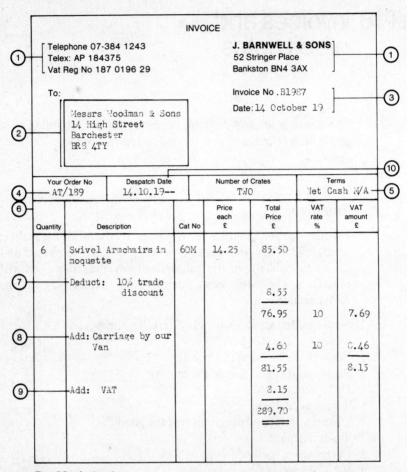

Fig. 38. An invoice

Quantities	
Quality and prices	
Extensions and totals	
Entered by	

The above is a typical rubber-stamp impression used for this purpose.

Value-added Tax

VAT is a tax on the supply of certain goods and services (including carriage) for which a standard rate of 8 per cent is at present payable. It is calculated on the discounted value of goods, i.e. after trade discount and, if necessary, cash discount, have been deducted. VAT is added to the net value of the goods to arrive at the net value of the invoice.

Pro forma invoices

Pro forma invoices are similar to ordinary invoices, containing such details as the quantity, price and a description of the goods, but they differ in two respects:

a The words *'pro forma'* are typed on the document. *Pro forma* means for form's sake.
b A *pro forma* invoice does not charge the addressee with the amount contained in it.

They are used for the following purposes:

1 To accompany goods sent out on approval or on consignment, and to inform the addressee of the price and charges expected should the goods be retained.
2 For a dealer who is contemplating the introduction of a new sales line, so that he can be given accurate and full particulars, which will show him if he can trade profitably. *Pro forma* invoices are, in these cases, really quotations.
3 For a manufacturer or dealer who is prepared to execute an order on payment of the invoice amount. This is normally done where the transaction is small, or where the buyers are unknown to the sellers or have not sent satisfactory references.
4 If the goods are being sent abroad, a *pro forma* invoice is required by the customs authorities for declaring the amount of the consignment.

Credit notes

Credit notes are used to rectify errors and remedy omissions caused by:

1 Goods being damaged or lost in transit.
2 An error being made in the price quoted in an invoice; and for the following purposes:
3 To return goods when the wrong quantity or type of articles has been sent.

Office routine for selling goods on credit

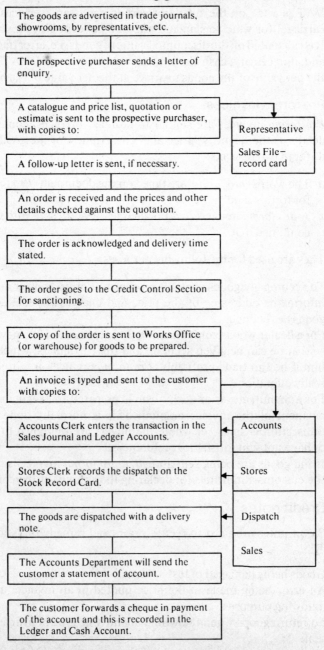

The goods are advertised in trade journals, showrooms, by representatives, etc.

The prospective purchaser sends a letter of enquiry.

A catalogue and price list, quotation or estimate is sent to the prospective purchaser, with copies to:

Representative

Sales File—record card

A follow-up letter is sent, if necessary.

An order is received and the prices and other details checked against the quotation.

The order is acknowledged and delivery time stated.

The order goes to the Credit Control Section for sanctioning.

A copy of the order is sent to Works Office (or warehouse) for goods to be prepared.

An invoice is typed and sent to the customer with copies to:

Accounts Clerk enters the transaction in the Sales Journal and Ledger Accounts.

Accounts

Stores Clerk records the dispatch on the Stock Record Card.

Stores

The goods are dispatched with a delivery note.

Dispatch

Sales

The Accounts Department will send the customer a statement of account.

The customer forwards a cheque in payment of the account and this is recorded in the Ledger and Cash Account.

4 For returning faulty goods or cancelling the charge for them.

When the errors or omissions are discovered, an adjustment is made by issuing a credit note. The correction must not be made on the invoice as the original details may already have been recorded in the accounts.

A credit note, illustrated in Fig. 39 (p. 111), is a statement of an allowance made by a seller for goods returned, overcharges, packing cases returned, short weight and price reductions. If the seller has to credit the buyer for any of these reasons and the charge made in the invoice is higher than it should be, he sends the buyer a credit note to inform him that he is being credited with the amount of the discrepancy. These are usually printed in red and can therefore be easily distinguished from other business documents.

If the seller has undercharged the buyer another invoice is usually issued to charge the buyer with the additional amount.

Questions

1 Write fully about the use of (a) a quotation; (b) a delivery note; (c) an invoice; (d) a credit note.

Consider these documents from the point of view of both the seller and the buyer.   (R.S.A.)

2 Explain briefly the following terms:
   a a tender;
   b a *pro forma* invoice.   (R.S.A.)

3 What purpose is served by (a) the advice note; (b) the credit note; and (c) the invoice? State the essential details to be shown on an invoice.   (R.S.A.)

4 You are employed as an invoice clerk for Amalgamated Engineers Ltd, and are required to draw up an invoice to J. Parker & Sons Ltd, 119 High Street, Coventry CO1 4AS, for the following items:

TWO Model 141 Filing Cabinets – Double Capacity with Lock in grey
TWO Model 121 Filing Cabinets – Standard with Lock in grey.

Refer to the price list on page 96 for the prices and other details. The cabinets were dispatched on 28 September 19... A trade discount of 15 per cent was allowed and the terms of payment were Net Cash within one month after delivery. Add £7 for carriage and packing.

5 One of the Model 141 Filing Cabinets (referred to in Question 4) was damaged in transit and had to be returned to Amalgamated Engineers Ltd on 10 October 19... Prepare the credit note which Amalgamated Engineers Ltd would have to send to J. Parker & Sons Ltd to record the return.

6 Write True or False against each of the following statements:

   a A credit note is used to rectify an error made on an invoice.
   b An invoice is a statement sent by a buyer to a seller giving particulars of goods purchased.
   c A *pro-forma* invoice may be used as an alternative to an invoice to charge the buyer with goods supplied.
   d VAT is a tax which is added to the net value of goods sold.

For additional practical questions, refer to Sections 4.2 and 4.3 of *Practical Office Exercises.*

CREDIT NOTE

No. C567

Telephone: 07-384 1243
Telex: AP 184375
VAT Reg No 187 0196 29

J. BARNWELL & SONS
52 Stringer Place
Bankston BN4 3AX
Date: 20 October 19--

To:

Messrs Woodman & Sons
14 High Street
Barchester
BR8 4TY

Invoice No: B1937   Dated: 14 October 19--

Quantity	Description	Cat No	Price each £	Total Price £	VAT rate %	VAT amount £
1	Swivel Armchair returned as damaged in transit	60M	14.25	14.25		
	Deduct: 10% trade discount			1.42		
				12.83	10	1.28
	Add: VAT			1.28		
				£14.11		

Fig. 39. A credit note (this document is normally printed in red)

Unit **19** Statements of account

Credit trade is usually conducted on the basis of monthly payments, and controlled by the use of statements of account. Their purpose and methods of preparation are described below.

At the end of the month, which may be any fixed date in the month, statements of account are issued by the accounts clerk showing the dates, the amounts of the invoices and credit notes and the total due. In credit transactions the buyer, because he makes several purchases from the same supplier, does not pay each invoice as it arrives. When an invoice is issued for goods supplied, the seller debits (or adds to the amount already owing) the amount in the buyer's account in the ledger; credit notes issued and cheques received are credited (or deducted) from the amount owing. The method of making entries in the ledger is illustrated as follows:

J. Smith Account				
19— Details Fo	Dr £	Cr £	Balance £	
	(Additions)	(Deductions)		
Invoices ⟶	→			
Credit notes ⟶		→		
Cheques and Discount ⟶		→		

When the buyer receives the monthly statement of account, he checks it with the invoices and credit notes received.

Statements are usually prepared by accounting machines or copywriter boards at the same time as the entries are made in the ledger and journal. This eases the situation at the end of the month, as the statements are ready for sending out immediately the last ledger posting for the month has been made.

A specimen statement is illustrated in Fig. 40.

STATEMENT

Telephone 07-384 1243
Telex: AP 184375
Vat Reg No 187 0196 29

J. BARNWELL & SONS
52 Stringer Place
Bankston BN4 3AX
Date 31 October 19 --

To

Messrs Woodman & Sons
14 High Street
Barchester BR8 4TY

Terms Net Cash M/A

Date 19--	Details	Ref. No.	Dr £		Cr £		Balance £	
Oct. 1	A/C Rendered						71	20
" 14	Sales	B1987	89	70			160	90
" 20	Returns	C567			14	11	146	79
" 21	Cash				71	20	75	59

The last amount in the balance column is the amount owing

Fig. 40. A statement of account

Discounts

Before payment is made, the accountant checks the statements received and deducts any cash discount.

Cash discount is an allowance made as a consideration for the prompt settlement of accounts within a stated period. The terms of cash discount are usually quoted on the invoice, e.g. $2\frac{1}{2}$ per cent monthly means that if the buyer pays the amount of the account not later than a month after the date of the statement, he is entitled to deduct a discount of $2\frac{1}{2}$ per cent. Cash discount should not be confused with trade discount.

Trade discount is an allowance from the invoice or list price of goods; it is deducted on the invoice and it does not depend on the time of payment. It is given as an allowance for a large order, an agent's profit or as a correction of a price in the catalogue.

Adding machines

A considerable amount of the work in an accounts office is concerned with the production of routine records, many of which can be compiled by adding and calculating machines. Machinery helps to speed up the production of accounting records and relieves the book-keeper of a great deal of routine work.

Adding/listing machines perform the functions not only of adding but in some cases of subtraction, multiplication and the printing of calculations on a tally roll. There are two principal types of adding/listing machine:

1 A small keyboard machine with ten keys only, as illustrated in Fig. 41. The clerk can be trained to use this type of machine by touch and,

Fig. 41. An adding/listing machine (*reproduced by permission of Addo Ltd*)

because of the small area of the keyboard, finds it is less fatiguing to operate. Calculations are made by depressing, in succession, the appropriate keys in the same order as the figures would be read.

2 A full keyboard machine which consists of over 100 keys. The advantages of this machine are that several keys can be depressed simultaneously instead of consecutively as on the small keyboard, the operator can actually see all the amounts set up on the keyboard before the crank is operated and mistakes can be corrected by depressing the correct keys, i.e. before the crank is operated.

Adding/listing machines may be used for checking statements, invoices, P.A.Y.E. records and many other routine adding and listing operations.

Questions

1 Explain the purpose of cash discount and trade discount and the circumstances under which each is given.

2 W. H. & Co. Ltd issued to wholesalers and large-scale retailers an illustrated catalogue accompanied by a circular stating that the printed prices were subject to a trade discount of $33\frac{1}{3}$ per cent and a cash discount of $2\frac{1}{2}$ per cent for payment within 14 days of the invoice date. Explain why W. H. & Co. Ltd use this method of pricing their goods, and state the amount paid for goods listed at £60, supplied on 16 February, and paid for one week later.   *(R.S.A.)*

3 On 1 February 19.., T. Draper, of High Street, Camberley owed £70 to the United Wholesalers Ltd, of Manchester. During the month of February Draper had the following transactions with the United Wholesalers Ltd:

			£
Feb. 10	Bought goods on credit	. . . . .	80
„ 17	Bought goods on credit	. . . . .	75
„ 22	Sent cheque in settlement of balance owing on 1 February less $2\frac{1}{2}$ per cent discount.		
„ 24	Received credit note for £10 for goods returned.		

Make out the document which Draper would receive at the end of the month from the United Wholesalers Ltd, in respect of these transactions. What are the functions of this document?   *(R.S.A.)*

4 Name three uses of the adding/listing machine.   *(R.S.A.)*

5 *a* What are the functions of the invoice and the statement in the sale of goods? Mention their similarities and their differences.

   b From the following details prepare a statement to be sent out on 30 April 197-, by J. W. Harrison Ltd, of 32 Bank Place, Reading, to H. Thompson, 26 Chorley Road, Lancaster.

197–

April 1   Balance owing by H. Thompson £55.

     4   Sold to H. Thompson 3 Bathroom Suites @ £85 each, less 20 per cent Trade Discount.

   14   Allowance to H. Thompson for bath damaged in transit £45.

   25   Cheque for £100 received from H. Thompson. Cash discount of £5 allowed.   *(R.S.A.)*

6   Answer the following questions on the Statement below:

a   What is the name of the supplier?
b   What is the reference number of the customer's account?
c   How much did the customer owe at the beginning of the period?
d   How much did the customer spend during the month of September?
e   How much did the customer pay during the period?
f   How much did the customer owe at the end of September?

STATEMENT

WILLIAMSON & CO. LTD

16 George Street

Bath

Mr F. Freeman
295 Portland Place
London, W.1
A/c 6/F/138

Date		Dr.	Cr.	Balance
197		£	£	£
July 1	Balance forward			2.40
10	Cash		2.40	
Sept. 18	Goods	17.37		
21	do.	5.91		
25	do.	29.18		
30	do.	51.77		
	Cash		20.50	
	Credit note		2.50	81.23

(R.S.A.)

7 In each of the two parts of this question, select the correct answer:

(i) Cash discount is an allowance for:

    a a reduction of a price in the catalogue;
    b payments made in cash by instalments;
    c a large order;
    d prompt settlement of an account within a stated period.

(ii) When commencing work on an adding machine, which should you do first:

    a enter the first amount;
    b enter the date;
    c take a total;
    d enter the account number?

For additional practical questions, refer to Section 5.1 of *Practical Office Exercises*.

Unit **20** Methods of payment

After checking the statements of account and deducting cash discount, the buyer sends a remittance to the seller. The cashier uses one of the following methods:

1 Registered cash ⎫
2 Postal order   ⎬ See Unit 7
3 Giro   ⎭
4 Cheque
5 Credit transfer

Current account

A current account is the usual account which a person has with a bank when he wishes to have the use of a cheque book and other bank facilities. Money is paid into a current account by the use of a paying-in book and withdrawals are made by cheque.

Deposit account

If a customer has some surplus money which he does not need to use immediately for making payments, he may invest it in a deposit account where it will earn interest. The bank may require a few days' notice of withdrawal, but this is not usually needed for small amounts. The money is not drawn out of a deposit account by cheque, but by submitting a withdrawal form.

Cheques

Cheques are a very common means of settling accounts because they are efficient, easy to prepare and safe to use. A cheque is a written order to a banker to pay a certain sum of money from the customer's current account to a person named or to bearer.

There are three persons involved when a cheque is made out:

1 The *drawer*: the person who signs the cheque and whose account will be debited (i.e. reduced by the amount of the cheque).

2 The *drawee*: the bank on which the cheque is drawn, i.e. the drawer's bank.

3 The *payee*: the person to whom the cheque is made payable.

The three parties concerned are shown on the cheque given in Fig.42.

Fig. 42. A cheque (*reproduced by permission of Midland Bank Ltd*)

Cheques should be written very carefully in ink. The amounts in writing and figures should agree, and both should be written to the left of the lines and in such a way as to make alteration difficult, if not impossible. The other details should not be omitted, especially the signature, for without this the cheque is valueless. If an alteration is made on a cheque, it should be confirmed by the drawer's signature being placed as near to the alteration as possible. The signature should be that ordinarily used and it must always remain the same to correspond with the specimen given to the banker when the account was opened. A line should be drawn through any blank spaces remaining after the words and figures have been filled in.

Two parallel lines put across the face of a cheque with or without the words '& Co.' provide an instruction to the banker upon whom the cheque is drawn to pay the amount through a bank only; he may not pay cash to the payee or holder unless the payee or holder is a banker. This type of crossing, as illustrated below, is called a 'general crossing'.

If the name of a banker is put between the transverse lines, the cheque is then payable only into an account at that bank or its agent; in this case the crossing is called 'special' *(see below).*

If the cashier wishes to ensure that a cheque may only be paid into the account of the person to whom it is made out, he writes the words 'a/c. Payee only' between the lines of the crossing; for example:

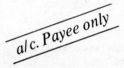

If the cashier possesses a book of crossed cheques and he wishes to draw out money for petty-cash purposes, he can 'open' the cheques by writing 'Pay Cash' and signing his name between the crossing lines.

The cheque illustrated in Fig. 42 is called an 'order cheque'; if the payee desires that someone else should receive the money, he can endorse the cheque, that is, write his name on the back of it. Thus if Mr X pays into his account a cheque made payable to Mr Y, it must have been endorsed by Mr Y.

It is not necessary to endorse cheques which are paid into a bank for the credit of the payee's account, i.e. when Mr X pays into his bank a cheque made payable to him. The payee's endorsement is required on cheques cashed across the counter of a bank.

If the word 'Bearer' is used instead of 'Order' the cheque is called a 'bearer cheque', and it is payable without endorsement to anyone who presents it.

As with other documents dealt with in this book, counterfoils are used as a means of keeping a brief record of the particulars contained on the cheques.

Paying-in book

The cashier is responsible for checking all remittances received, recording them and paying them into a current account at the bank. The bank supplies paying-in slips or a paying-in book for the purpose

Fig. 43. A paying-in slip
(*reproduced by permission of Midland Bank Ltd*)

of recording payments made into an account. Each page is divided into two or three parts by perforated lines. The bank clerk checks the cash, etc., and ticks off the amounts on the slip, checks the additions and initials the counterfoil which he hands back to the customer. The exact details of the money paid in (cash, notes, cheques, etc.) have to be recorded on the counterfoil (see Fig. 43).

The bank statement

Periodically the bank supplies a statement which contains a record of all the transactions which have taken place between the customer and itself involving the receipt and payment of money. The balance of the bank statement is the amount the bank has in hand of the customer's money. A specimen bank statement is illustrated in Fig. 44.

Receipts

Receipts are now seldom given when payment is made by cheque, mainly as a result of the Cheques Act, 1957, which established that a cheque passing through a bank provided sufficient evidence of payment. Receipts are, however, issued for other forms of payment and in some cases for cheques. Some firms require the acknowledgement on the invoice or statement, but it is more general to have loose receipt forms or books with carbon duplicates or counterfoils.

A receipt should contain the date, name of the remitter, amount in words and figures, a reference to the account or reason for the payment, and the signature of the payee. If the amount is not in settlement, the words 'On account' should be inserted.

The counterfoil should be filled in for reference. Receipts should

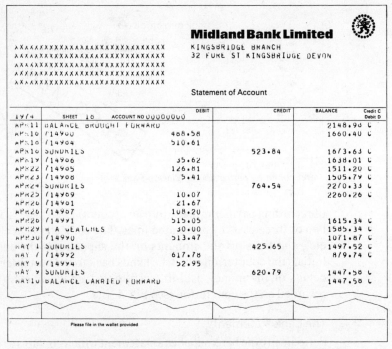

Fig. 44. A bank statement (*reproduced by permission of Midland Bank Ltd*)

be filed for at least six years, after which time simple contract debts are 'statute barred', i.e. the courts will not enforce payment.

If an accounting machine or a copywriter board is employed, the receipt, proof sheet and bank paying-in slip are written simultaneously, which saves time and is much more accurate than if the entries are made separately. The payments are then recorded in the sales ledger and on the statement from the proof sheet (or cash-book page).

Standing orders

If a payment has to be made regularly for items such as insurance premiums or hire-purchase repayments, the bank can be asked to make the payment from a current account and the customer does not have the trouble of remembering the dates and writing and posting the cheques. The instructions for this service, known as a standing order, must be given to the banker in writing, as must the request to cease such payments.

Credit transfers

A credit-transfer system can be used for the payment of several creditors without the drawer having to prepare separate cheques for each amount. A list, containing the names of the creditors and the amounts to be paid, is sent to the bank together with one cheque for the total amount. The bank then arranges for credit slips to be sent out to the creditors through their banks. The creditor must, in the first place, give his written authority for payment to be made by credit transfer.

This system is also suitable for an individual who wishes to transfer money from a bank, irrespective of whether he has an account there, to a bank account of a person or business whom he wishes to pay. If the remitter does not have a bank account, the amount to be paid is handed over the counter of a bank, together with a completed credit transfer form and a small fee. The bank clerk will initial and stamp the counterfoil and return it to the remitter as a receipt for the money.

A comparison of cheques and credit transfers

Cheque	Credit transfer
1. Sent direct to payee by drawer and is more personal.	Sent to drawer's bank who send it, via the clearing house, to the payee's bank.
2. Arrives next day by post.	Takes longer to reach payee.
3. A separate cheque is required for each creditor.	One cheque is used for several creditors – saving expense in envelopes and postage.
4. Payee must pay the cheque into his bank.	This is already in the bank and payee does not have to take any action at all, providing a safer method of payment.
5. Drawer must have a bank account, but payee need not.	Drawer need not have a bank account, but payee must.

Credit Cards

A bank credit-card system enables a person to buy goods on credit at shops, garages, hotels, etc. which have agreed to take part in the scheme. The individual who applies for a credit card is notified of his credit limit, which is the maximum amount he can owe to the bank at any time. A card holder is also entitled to withdraw up to £25 or a sum not exceeding his credit limit, without prior notice, from any branch of the bank. The scheme operates in the following way:

1　The purchaser presents his credit card when ordering goods or services.
2　The supplier makes out a sales voucher in duplicate which is signed by the purchaser and has an impression inserted on it from the credit card.
3　The supplier retains the copy of the sales voucher and issues the purchaser with the second copy.
4　The supplier deposits all the sales vouchers he has collected at a branch of the bank and is credited with the amounts less a discount charge.
5　The bank forwards the sales vouchers to the credit-card centre.
6　The purchaser receives a monthly statement from the credit-card centre and provided he pays the amount owing not later than twenty-five days after the date on the statement, no charge is made.

Cheque Cards

A cheque card does not entitle the holder to credit, but is a card of authority which makes the cheque a more readily acceptable means of payment as it is an assurance to the trader that there is no risk in accepting it (up to the value of £50) from the holder. A cheque card also entitles the holder to cash cheques up to £50 at any branch of the bank without prior arrangements being made.

Cash Cards

Cash cards may be issued to bank customers to enable them to withdraw cash from cash dispensers (see Fig. 45) at any time of the day or night when banks are closed. When a customer is issued with a cash card he is told his personal number, which he must remember as it is not recorded on his card for security reasons. To obtain cash the card has to be inserted in a cash dispenser and the personal number tapped out on the machine buttons. This instructs the machine to issue ten £1 notes and return the card for future use.

Questions

1　You have two personal accounts at your bank – a current account and a deposit account. Say briefly but clearly what steps you will take:

a　to withdraw £20 from your current account;
b　to withdraw £20 from your deposit account.　　　　*(R.S.A.)*

Fig. 45. A cash dispenser (*reproduced by permission of Midland Bank Ltd*)

2   Some banks are now issuing credit cards to their customers. Explain how these are used, mentioning their advantages.   *(R.S.A.)*

3   What services do banks render to the businessman? Answer as fully as possible.   *(R.S.A.)*

4   What is meant by 'standing orders' as a method of payment? For what purposes are they used?   *(R.S.A.)*

5   *a*   Give two instances when uncrossed cheques could be used.
    b   How would you 'open' a crossed cheque?   *(R.S.A.)*

6   What are the following documents and in what circumstances would they be used:
    a   credit note;
    b   credit transfer;
    c   quotation;
    d   advice note?
      Say what steps an accounts clerk would take on receipt of (*a*) and notification of (*b*).   *(R.S.A.)*

7   Bankers offer their customers the use of both current and deposit accounts. Explain each of these services, pointing out their similarities and their differences.   *(R.S.A.)*

8   Various crossings are used on cheques. Give examples of three, and state the effect of each. *(R.S.A.)*

9   How would you turn the following into cash:
    a   your salary which has been paid by credit transfer;
    b   an open cheque? *(R.S.A.)*

10 *a*   What is a bank-credit card?
    b   How would the card be used by:
          (i)   the customer;
          (ii) the seller? *(R.S.A.)*

11 How would you withdraw £20 from your bank account when using a branch different from that where your account is held? *(R.S.A.)*

12 Select the correct answer below:
    A banker's standing order is:
    a   an order to a banker to pay a fixed sum at regular intervals to a named person;
    b   an order to supply new stationery to the bank;
    c   an order to settle your overdraft;
    d   an order for collection of a customer's debts. *(R.S.A.)*

For additional practical questions, refer to Sections 6.2, 6.3, 6.4 and 6.5 of *Practical Office Exercises.*

Unit **21** The petty-cash book

In the previous unit the cashier's responsibilities for the payment of remittances into the bank and the preparation of cheques were explained; in this unit we shall see how the cashier deals with the payment of sundry expenses.

The petty-cash book, as illustrated in Fig. 46, is used for the entry of small items of expenditure, chiefly to save the inclusion of trifling items in the business cash book. A round sum (known as the 'Imprest') is allocated for a period, at the end of which the petty cashier submits his book to the cashier and obtains cash, or a cheque to be cashed, for the exact amount expended; he then starts all his periods with the same amount. The petty cashier should obtain vouchers or receipts for all payments made. At any time in the period the total of the cash plus the current month's vouchers should equal the amount of the imprest. Note the specimen voucher in Fig. 47. The vouchers should be numbered as they are received and the number entered in the special column in the petty-cash book; they should then be filed numerically in a loose-leaf file. The analysis columns of the petty-cash book can be varied to

Dr   Fig. 46. A petty-cash book   **Cr**

Date	Details	Fo.	Receipts	Date	Details	V.N.	Total	Postage	Cleaning	Stationery	Travelling	Office Expenses	VAT
19--			£	19--			£	£	£	£	£	£	£
May 1	To Cash	CB.1	50.00	May 1	By stamps	11	5.00	5.00					
				May 2	By Paper towels	12	1.10					1.00	0.10
				May 5	By Ink	13	0.21			0.19			0.02
				May 8	By Telegram	14	0.68	0.68					
				May 9	By Cleaning materials	15	0.43		0.39				0.04
				May 11	By Shorthand notebook	16	0.26			0.24			0.02
				May 12	By Travelling expenses	17	3.22				3.22		
				May 15	By Taxi fare	18	0.62				0.62		
				May 16	By Blotting paper	19	0.27			0.25			0.02
				May 17	By Milk	20	0.62					0.62	
				May 19	By String	21	0.24			0.22			0.02
				May 22	By First Aid equipment	22	0.57					0.52	0.05
				May 24	By Donation to charity	23	0.25					0.25	
				May 25	By Cleaning materials	24	0.32		0.29				0.03
				May 29	By Office Manager (Entertaining)	25	3.05					2.77	0.28
							16.84	5.68	0.68	0.90	3.84	5.16	0.58
			50.00	May 31	By Balance	c/d	33.16	L.1	L.2	L.3	L.4	L.5	L.6
							50.00						
June 1	To Balance	b/d	33.16										
June 1	To Cash	CB.2	16.84										

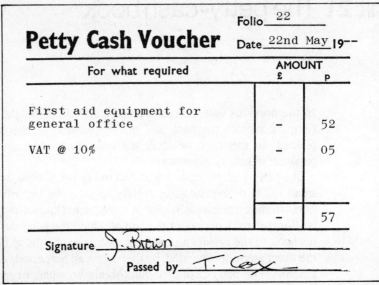

Fig. 47. A petty-cash voucher

suit the individual requirements of an office. Each of these columns represents an account in the ledger and at the end of the month the total amount in the column is transferred to the ledger account. If VAT has been paid it is entered in the VAT column as part of the analysis of the total payment.

Questions

1 Explain the Imprest system of keeping petty cash.

2 Enter the following items in a petty cash book:

19..	VAT included (£)	Total payments (£)
Jan 2 Postage stamps	–	0.75
Adhesive tape	0.02	0.22
String	0.01	0.11
Ink	0.01	0.11
,, 3 Teas	–	0.40
Newspapers	–	0.20
Sharpening scissors	0.02	0.25
,, 4 Envelopes	0.06	0.65
,, 5 Wrapping paper	0.07	0.73
,, 6 Accounts books	0.09	0.99
Rubber stamp	0.08	0.88

Extend the items into the analysis columns, make the addition and deduct the total spent from the amount of cash received (£10) and show the balance.

3   *a*   From the following details prepare the petty-cash book of M. Stocks to show in columnar form the expenses of Office Expenses and Salaries.

19 . .		£
May	1 Balance in hands of the petty cashier	1.87
,,	1 The balance is made up to £15	
,,	4 Paid office expenses (VAT included £0.30)	3.30
,,	6 Paid office expenses (VAT included £0.10)	1.10
,,	8 Paid salaries	3.50
,,	12 Paid office expenses (VAT included £0.06)	0.66
,,	16 Paid salaries	3.75

  b   How would you deal with the balance of unexpended petty cash at 16 May?

4   Rule up a petty-cash book with analysis columns, and enter the following items:

197–		£
March 2	Balance in hand	5.13
	Received from cashier	14.88
	Bought stamps	3.00
,, 3	Postage on parcel	0.48
	Bus fares	0.29
	String and gum (VAT included £0.03)	0.29
,, 4	Bought pencils (VAT included £0.04)	0.44
	Surcharge on letters	0.08
	Tea and milk for office teas	0.54

Balance the book on 5 March.   *(R.S.A.)*

5   Draw up and complete a petty-cash voucher for the pencils bought in Question 4.
                                                         (R.S.A.)

6   You are asked to take charge of petty cash controlled by the *imprest system,* and to record receipts and payments in a petty-cash book, using *analysis columns.* Explain clearly and fully what is meant by the words in italics.
                                                          (R.S.A.)

7   You are responsible for petty cash in your office and for the purchase and payment of certain items. Describe fully and clearly what method of recording you would use, giving details of any documents or book-keeping that you would suggest, explaining the terms you use in your answer.   *(R.S.A.)*

8   In a petty-cash book, why are payments entered at least twice, once in the total column and again under an appropriate heading?   *(R.S.A.)*

9   *a* Office sundries include such items as typewriter ribbons and pencil erasers. List four others.

    b Name the books and equipment necessary for the efficient operation of a petty-cash system.

    c Make out a petty-cash voucher referring to the sum of £1.20 paid for window cleaning in the office this week.   *(R.S.A.)*

10   Select the correct answer below:

Imprest is:

    a a method of rectifying mistakes in a balance sheet;

    b a system of keeping petty cash;

    c a form used for claiming petty cash;

    d a system for calculating income tax.   *(R.S.A.)*

For additional practical questions, refer to Section 6.6 of *Practical Office Exercises.*

Unit 22 Payment of wages

The clerk in a wages office has to handle a large number of different forms and cards concerning employment times and rates, tax deductions, National Insurance contributions, superannuation contributions, pay, etc. A selection of the documents commonly used is explained and illustrated in this unit.

Time cards

Where wages are being paid on a time basis, there must be some form of written record of the time worked. If, however, the wages or salaries are calculated on a weekly or monthly basis, the same degree of checking is not essential, but clocking-in cards may still be used to encourage punctuality in attendance. This is an easy method of checking the regular attendance of staff because all late or irregular times are shown in red.

Time-recording clocks are employed for the purpose of registering the time the employees start work and the time they leave their place of employment. Each employee is given a time card, as illustrated in Fig. 48, containing a record of the time worked for a week. As the employee enters his place of employment, he takes his card out of a steel rack and drops it into a slot in the time recorder and presses a handle. Many time clocks are automatic, the card being stamped as soon as it is inserted; the employee uses one hand only for this operation so that even if he is carrying a bag or parcel in the other hand, he can still use the machine easily and quickly. An impression of the day and time is printed in the appropriate space on the card. The cards are arranged in racks so that the top edges of the cards are visible, showing the works numbers or names of the employees.

At the end of the week the completed cards are collected by the wages clerks and form the basis for calculating the gross pay. The total hours worked will be added up and multiplied by the rate per hour. The wages clerk is then ready to calculate the amount of deductions in order to arrive at a net wage.

The amount of the employee's share of the National Insurance contribution is deducted from his gross pay, together with a superannuation-

| No. 78 | \multicolumn{4}{c}{**AMALGAMATED ENGINEERS LTD.**} |

Name *P.H. Johnson*

Week Ending *16 April 19*

	Morning		Afternoon		Evening		Total
	In	Out	In	Out	In	Out	
M	8 00	12 00	13 00	17 00			8
TU	8 00	12 02	12 59	17 33			8½
W	7 59	12 01	13 00	17 31			8½
TH	7 58	12 00	12 57	17 32	18 00	20 30	11
FR	8 10	12 02	12 59	17 30			8½
SA	8 00	12 00					4
TOTAL							48½

	Hours	Rate		£	
Ordinary Time	42	£1		42	00
Overtime	6½	£1.50		9	75
\multicolumn{4}{r}{TOTAL GROSS WAGES}	51	75

Fig. 48. A time card

scheme contribution if one is payable. Another deduction which the employer must make from his employee's gross pay is income tax. The employee pays his income tax as he earns his money; the amount of tax is related to his actual earnings and the weekly or monthly deduction of tax is adjusted to meet any variations. All employees who receive an earned income which exceeds the minimum on which tax is payable have to pay income tax.

Tax-deduction cards

The amount of tax to be deducted from an employee's pay is calculated on a tax-deduction card (see Fig. 49). The card is completed as follows:

a Enter the amount of gross pay in column (2).

b Add (*a*) to the total of all previous payments made to the employee since 6 April and enter it in column (3).

c Calculate the amount of 'free pay' and enter this in column (4). The wages clerk refers to Table A (free-pay table) in the tax tables.

d Subtract the 'free pay' in (*c*) from the total gross pay to date in (*b*) to arrive at the amount of 'taxable pay', which is entered in column (5).

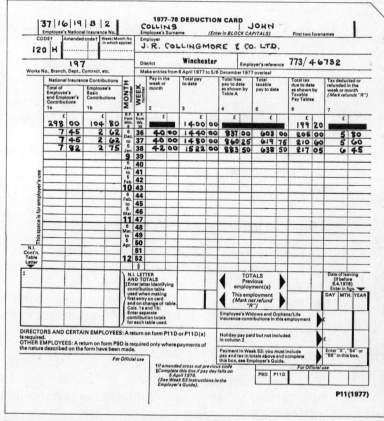

Fig. 49. A tax-deduction card (*Crown copyright. Reproduced by permission of the Controller, H.M.S.O.*)

e Calculate the total tax due to date by referring to the amount of 'taxable pay' in the taxable-pay tables and enter this sum in column (6).

f Subtract the amount of tax already deducted from the total tax due to date in (*e*), giving the amount to be entered in column (7). This is the amount of tax to be deducted from the employee's gross pay.

g If the employee has worked a short week or has been absent, the amount of total tax shown in the tax tables may be less than the tax already deducted, and the wages clerk will have to refund the difference to the employee. The amount of any refund is entered in column (7) with the initial 'R'.

h The total of National Insurance payable by employer and employee is entered in column (1a) and the employee's contribution is entered in column (1b).

The employer returns the completed tax-deduction cards to the Collector of Taxes at the end of the tax year.

The amount of tax to be deducted by the employer each payday depends upon:

1 The employee's code number – listed on his tax-deduction card – which represents his income-tax allowances and indicates the amount of free pay on which tax is not payable.
2 His total gross pay since the beginning of the tax year.
3 The total amount of tax deducted on previous days in the current tax year.

National Insurance contributions

The contributions payable for National Insurance are also related to gross earnings and are collected with income tax by the P.A.Y.E. method. Employees over school-leaving age and under 65 (60 for women) pay a standard-rate contribution of 6·5 per cent of their earnings and the employer pays 12·0 per cent of the employee's earnings, within a specified range of earnings to be determined from time to time. Reduced rates may be payable by certain married women and most widows entitled to the National Insurance widows' benefits. An employer may calculate contributions by using the percentages quoted above or he may refer to contribution tables supplied by the Department of Health and Social Security.

National Insurance contributions are entered on the tax-deduction card (P11) and deducted from gross pay, as explained in (*h*) above.

The employer is responsible for making monthly payments to the Collector of Taxes for all of his employees who contribute to the scheme, together with the income tax collected.

National Insurance contributions provide the employee with two pensions: a basic retirement pension and an additional state pension. The second pension can come either from the state or from a firm's own pension scheme for those who have contracted out. In addition to pensions the contributions entitle the employee to receive cash benefits for unemployment, sickness, maternity, widowhood and death.

Wages sheets

The gross pay and total deductions are entered on a wages sheet or pay roll which contains a list of all employees, arranged alphabetically or under departments. Accounting machines may be used to compile the wages sheet in conjunction with the employee's earning-record sheet, the pay slip for the employee and the pay envelope. In very large organizations wages sheets are prepared by punched-card or electronic-computer processes.

Office procedure for the payment of wages in cash

1 Clock cards are sorted into department and clock-number order, checked for times and hours are totalled.
2 Hours are priced, extended and added up to arrive at GROSS PAY, which is entered.
3 National Insurance contributions are calculated and entered.
4 Income tax is calculated (as indicated on pages 133-4) and entered.
5 The fixed deductions, such as social club, savings, etc. are entered (if they have not already been prepared by addressing machine).
6 Total deductions are added up and subtracted from gross pay (as in 2) to arrive at NET PAY which is entered.

These entries are made on the following documents:
a Tax-deduction card or employee's pay-record sheet;
b pay roll;
c pay advice slip.

7 Total the wages-sheet columns, cross cast and prove the totals.
8 'Coining' of the net wages, i.e. the number of coins and notes required for each employee is calculated and totalled.

9 Pay envelopes are prepared (if aperture envelopes are not used).
10 Cashier issues a cheque for net pay.
11 The money is collected from the bank.
12 Money and pay slips are inserted in the pay envelopes.
13 The contents are checked by a second person.
14 A cheque is sent (monthly) to the Collector of Taxes for P.A.Y.E. and National Insurance contributions.

Payment of wages

The following methods of payment may be used for wages:

1 Cash.
2 Cheque.
3 Credit transfer or Giro.
4 Postal order.

Employers' guides

Employers' guides are available on the following subjects:

1 Pay as You Earn.
2 National Insurance contributions.

   Copies of these handbooks should be available in all wages departments for reference purposes.

Questions

1 What deductions must be made, by law, from an employee's pay?
2 What is meant by:
   a P.A.Y.E. code numbers; and
   b tax-deduction tables?
3 a (i) Describe three methods of payment by which an employer could pay wages.
      (ii) Explain the disadvantages to an employee of one of these methods.
   b (i) Name two compulsory deductions which are taken from wages.
      (ii) Explain the purpose of one of these deductions.   *(R.S.A.)*
4 Under the P.A.Y.E. system, on what does the amount of tax to be deducted depend?
5 You are responsible for the preparation of wages for hourly-paid workers.
   a List the items of information required for the calculation of wages.
   b State the documents which must be kept in the wages department.
   c Set out in the correct order a system for the preparation of wages.   *(R.S.A.)*

6 State briefly what is meant by:
  a P.A.Y.E. code numbers;
  b tax-deduction tables. *(R.S.A.)*

7 Give three methods of payment for wages. Explain fully the procedure in each case, mentioning the advantages and disadvantages. *(R.S.A.)*

8 A business concern employs workmen on a distant site which causes them to live away from home for fairly long periods. Describe fully the method you would suggest for sending their wages. *(R.S.A.7*

9 What is meant by the following terms and abbreviations? Answer as fully as possible.
Trade discount, P.A.Y.E., C.O.D., poundage, crossed cheque. *(R.S.A.)*

10 Pair the following words, e.g. if you consider that (*a*) in the first column pairs with (*c*) in the second column, write (*c*) against (*a*):

  a Income tax   *a* Imprest
  b Bank   *b* C.O.D.
  c Petty cash   *c* P.A.Y.E.
  d Post Office   *d* Credit card

For additional practical questions, refer to Sections 7.1 and 7.2 of *Practical Office Exercises.*

Section D:
Books of reference in common use

Reference book	Synopsis of contents
A.B.C. Coach and Bus Guide	Times of coach and bus services.
A.B.C. Railway Guide	Times of departure and arrival of trains between London (or the town of issue) and the station of destination. Gives also fares, counties, populations, distances from London and early closing days.
A.B.C. Shipping Guide *Lloyd's Register of Shipping* }	Shipping details, including times.
A.B.C. World Airways Guide	Details of air services.
Army List (similar lists for Air Force and Navy)	Officers, regiments, etc.
Automobile Association Members' Handbook (or *Royal Automobile Club Guide and Handbook*)	Services offered to members, detailed maps of Great Britain, brief details of towns, including county, population, early closing day, appointed garages and hotels.
British Rail Timetables	Routes of trains and the names of all stations at which they stop. Also boat services connected with British Rail.
Crockford's Clerical Directory	Clergymen of the Church of England, their parishes and livings, etc.
Cyclopaedia of Initials and Abbreviations	The meaning of initials and abbreviations in common use.

Reference book	Synopsis of contents
Dictionary	Words and their spellings, meanings, derivations, pronunciations, etc.
Directory of Directors	Directors and their companies.
Gazetteer	Spelling and situation of towns, counties, etc.
Hansard	Verbatim reports of Parliament.
Kelly's Directory of Manufacturers and Merchants	Manufacturers and suppliers.
Medical Directory	Qualified medical practitioners.
Municipal Year Book and Public Utilities Directory	Areas, populations, rates and names of chief officers for local authorities in England and Wales.
Newspaper Press Directory (or Willing's Press Guide)	Newspapers, trade journals, etc.
Pears Cyclopaedia	Dictionary, gazetteer, ready reckoner, legal data, synonyms and antonyms, office compendium, etc.
Post Office Guide	Postal, telephone and telegraphic facilities including inland and overseas postal rates, methods of posting, savings, remittance and other services.
Ready Reckoner	A quick means of arriving at answers to calculations involving multiplication, discounts, percentages, etc.
Roget's Thesaurus of English Words and Phrases	The meaning of words; synonyms and antonyms; idioms and phrases.
Stock Exchange Official Year Book	Companies, securities and other company financial data.

Reference book	Synopsis of contents
Street Directory	Names of streets and the responsible occupiers of each house, office, shop and flat. Trades and professions are also listed.
Telephone Directory	Names, addresses and telephone numbers of subscribers. Trades and professions are also listed in the yellow pages.
Titles and Forms of Address (Black)	For ascertaining forms of address.
Whitaker's Almanack	The calendar year, world affairs, British and foreign embassies, United Kingdom—Sovereigns, the Royal Family, Peerage, Cabinet Ministers, Members of Parliament, Bank of England, Law Courts, Churches. The order of precedence in Great Britain. Statistical information. United Nations, Nobel Prize Winners. Literature, Music, Poetry, Drama, Art, Sport, etc.
Who's Who	Biographies of living eminent people.

Questions

1 From which reference books would you obtain the following information:
  a times of air services from London to Edinburgh;
  b instructions for sending an overseas telegram;
  c a list of signs used for correcting proofs;
  d a synonym for any word?   *(R.S.A.)*

2 Where would you find the following information:

  a a series of multiplication tables of sums of money;
  b the actual position in a town of a given address;
  c a list of traders carrying on the same trade in a given area;
  d the position of a small town in a foreign country;
  e detailed information regarding the movements of shipping?   *(R.S.A.)*

3   Where would you find the following information:

   a how to address an ambassador;
   b the name of the head of a government department;
   c official reports of proceedings in parliament?   *(R.S.A.)*

4   Where would you look for the following information:

   a the title of a member of the Peerage;
   b the times of trains from Manchester to Hull;
   c the cost of sending a parcel by airmail to Nigeria;
   d the name and address of a hotel in Bristol?   *(R.S.A.)*

5   What information would you find in:

   a a ready-reckoner;
   b *Who's Who*?

6   What information is contained in the following books of reference:

   a *Who's Who*;
   b *The Post Office Guide*;
   c A dictionary;
   d *Crockford's Clerical Directory*?   *(R.S.A.)*

7   What information would you expect to find in the following books:

   a *Roget's Thesaurus*;
   b an AA or RAC handbook;
   c a railway timetable;
   d *Hansard*?   *(R.S.A.)*

8   What four books of reference would you suggest as being most valuable in an office? Give your reasons.   *(R.S.A.)*

9   Rewrite the following list, putting the names of the persons next to the reference books which would contain information about them:

Rev. J. M. Jones	*Medical Directory*
M. B. Davies, M.D.	*Law List*
Sir John Dunn, Q.C.	*Crockford's Clerical Directory*
Rt Hon. Sir Alec Groves	*Municipal Year Book*
City Treasurer, Liverpool	*Who's Who* *(R.S.A.)*

10   In each of the two parts of this question, select the correct answer:

   (i) *Hansard* is:
      a a list of people holding public office;
      b a reference book listing English words and phrases;
      c an official report of Parliamentary debates;
      d a list of prominent business men.

(ii) The names of all Members of Parliament may be obtained from a current
      copy of:

a   *Who's Who* ;
b   *Hansard* ;
c   *Roget's Thesaurus* ;
d   *Whitaker's Almanack.*   *(R.S.A.)*

For additional practical questions, refer to Section 2.9 of *Practical Office
Exercises.*

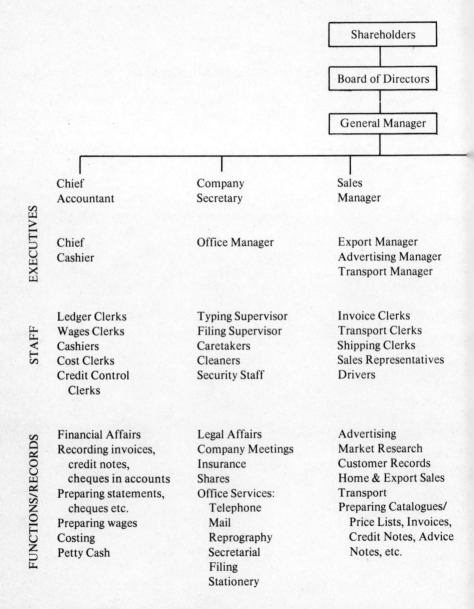

		Shareholders	
		Board of Directors	
		General Manager	
EXECUTIVES	Chief Accountant	Company Secretary	Sales Manager
	Chief Cashier	Office Manager	Export Manager Advertising Manager Transport Manager
STAFF	Ledger Clerks Wages Clerks Cashiers Cost Clerks Credit Control Clerks	Typing Supervisor Filing Supervisor Caretakers Cleaners Security Staff	Invoice Clerks Transport Clerks Shipping Clerks Sales Representatives Drivers

FUNCTIONS/RECORDS	Financial Affairs
	Recording invoices,
	   credit notes,
	   cheques in accounts
	Preparing statements,
	   cheques etc.
	Preparing wages
	Costing
	Petty Cash
		Legal Affairs
		Company Meetings
		Insurance
		Shares
		Office Services:
		   Telephone
		   Mail
		   Reprography
		   Secretarial
		   Filing
		   Stationery
			Advertising
			Market Research
			Customer Records
			Home & Export Sales
			Transport
			Preparing Catalogues/
			   Price Lists, Invoices,
			   Credit Notes, Advice
			   Notes, etc.

Note: Typists, secretaries and general clerks are attached to all departments.

Section E:
Business organization

The organization chart brings together the various office functions and business documents introduced in this book and shows how they are organized and the staff who are responsible for them in a typical firm:

Chief Buyer	Personnel Manager	Production Manager
Buyers	Employment Officer Training Officer Welfare Officer	Chief Engineer Chief Designer

Order Clerks
Stock Control
  Clerks
	Canteen Staff
	Nurses
		Engineers
		Factory Operatives
		Despatch Clerks
		Production Control
		  Clerks
		Draughtsmen

Purchase of goods
  and materials
Preparing orders
Stock records
Suppliers Records
	Recruitment,
	  Employment and
	  Dismissal of Staff
	Staff Records
	Welfare
	Training
		Production of Goods
		Quality Control
		Design and
		  Development
		Work Study
		Stores
		Despatch of Goods
		Maintenance of
		  Equipment
		Preparing Goods
		  Received Notes

Questions

1 A firm employs the following personnel:

There is a Managing Director to whom the General Manager and two Senior Executives are accountable. Each of the Senior Executives has a secretary. There are three Managers:

Personnel, with a shorthand-typist and two clerks.
Production, with a staff of one shorthand-typist and two clerks.
Company Secretary, with a staff of three filing clerks, three copy typists, three shorthand-typists and two wages clerks.
The Personnel Manager reports to one Senior Executive.
The Production Manager reports to the other Senior Executive.
The Company Secretary reports to the General Manager.

Make out an organization chart, showing clearly the lines of authority. *(R.S.A.)*

2 The organization chart below is of a typical medium-sized manufacturing company. Extend the chart for each department to show the category of staff under each manager's control and the type of work for which his department would be responsible. The Transport Manager's department has been completed as a guide. *(R.S.A.)*

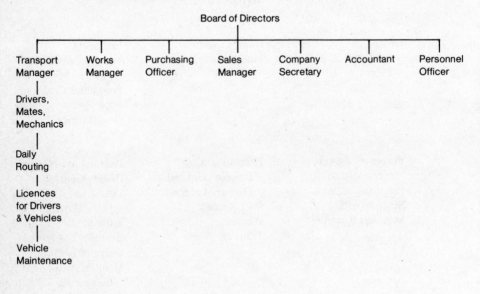

Board of Directors

Transport Manager — Works Manager — Purchasing Officer — Sales Manager — Company Secretary — Accountant — Personnel Officer

Transport Manager
│
Drivers, Mates, Mechanics
│
Daily Routing
│
Licences for Drivers & Vehicles
│
Vehicle Maintenance

3   Allocate the following under the appropriate heading of the three divisions
    given below.

DEPARTMENTAL HEAD	MEMBER OF DEPARTMENT'S STAFF	ACTIVITY OR DOCUMENT
e.g. Accountant	Ledger clerk	Posting invoices

Sales Manager, Transport Manager, <u>Accountant</u>, Personnel Officer, Purchasing
Officer, Works Manager, representative, <u>ledger clerk</u>, recruitment, typing
orders, driver, call sheets, <u>posting invoices</u>, factory operative, licences, personnel clerk, piece work, order clerk.

The items underlined are correctly set out as an example.   *(R.S.A.)*

4   Draw a chart to show the organization of a company into departments. *(R.S.A.)*

5   In each of the four parts of this question, select the correct answer:

   (i) The Personnel Manager of a large firm is responsible for:

   a   recruitment of all staff;
   b   insurance of company vehicles;
   c   payment of wages;
   d   publicity and advertising.

   (ii) In a large firm the payment of invoices is the responsibility of:

   a   the Chief Accountant;
   b   the Transport Manager;
   c   the Sales Manager;
   d   the Advertising Manager.

   (iii) In a large firm the function of seeking quotations is the responsibility of:

   a   the Sales Manager;
   b   the Production Controller;
   c   the Purchasing Manager;
   d   the Chief Engineer.   *(R.S.A.)*

Index